Content Yet Contending

Jude

Daniel R. Hyde

EP BOOKS

1st Floor Venture House, 6 Silver Court, Watchmead, Welwyn Garden City, UK, AL7 1TS

web: www.epbooks.org

e-mail: sales@epbooks.org

EP books are distributed in the USA by:

JPL Fulfillment

3741 Linden Avenue Southeast,

Grand Rapids, MI 49548

orders@jplbooks.com

Tel: 877.683.6935

Unless otherwise indicated, all Scripture quotations are from **The Holy Bible, English Standard Version**, copyright © 2001 by Crossway Bibles, a division of Good News Publishers. Used by permission. All rights reserved.

First published 2017

British Library Cataloguing in Publication Data available

ISBN: 978–1–78397–175–6

Content Yet Contending rightly spotlights the small and often overlooked Epistle of Jude, which has momentous relevance to the church in our doctrinally confused and indifferent times. Danny Hyde's exposition is a fitting combination of the pastoral and polemical—since protecting Jesus' sheep from Satan's attractive but lethal lies demands that their shepherds discerningly expose and resist any and all spiritual predators.

—Dr. Dennis E. Johnson, Professor of Practical Theology, Westminster Seminary California, Escondido, CA

Jude is a small letter with a big message for the church. Danny Hyde's expository commentary on Jude is an accessible and thoughtful guide to a New Testament book that is not as well known as it should be. With clarity and boldness, Hyde helps us to see the ongoing relevance of Jude's message for the contemporary church—exhorting us to remain faithful to the teaching of Scripture; calling us to godly living; and warning us against false teachers in the church. *Content Yet Contending* is a welcome cure for complacency and a strong stimulus to persevere in the Christian life. I warmly commend it.

—Dr. Guy Waters, James M. Baird, Jr. Professor of New Testament, Reformed Theological Seminary, Jackson, MS

To all faithful and godly servants of the Word:
You are afflicted, but know you are not crushed;
You are perplexed, but know you are not driven to despair;
You are persecuted, but know you are not forsaken;
You are struck down, but know you are not destroyed;
You are dying to self with Christ, but know you are bringing
life to the dead.
From 2 Corinthians 4:8–12

Contents

Abbreviations

BC—Belgic Confession (1561)

Calvin, *Commentary*—*A Harmony of the Gospels Matthew, Mark and Luke, Volume 3, and the Epistles of James and Jude*, trans. A. W. Morrison, eds. David W. Torrance and Thomas F. Torrance, Calvin's New Testament Commentaries, 12 vols. Grand Rapids, Mich.: Eerdmans, 1972.

Calvin, *Exposition*—"John Calvin's 1542 Exposition of Jude," trans. Thomas and Geneviève Reid. *Kerux: The Journal of Northwest Theological Seminary* 26/3 (2011): 3–15.

CD—Canons of Dort (1618–1619)

HC—Heidelberg Catechism (1563)

Luther, *Sermons*—Martin Luther, "Sermons on the Epistle of St. Jude," trans. Martin H. Bertram, in *Luther's Works: Volume 30, Catholic Epistles*, ed. Jaroslav Pelikan (Saint Louis, MO: Concordia Publishing House, 1967).

Manton, *Jude*—Thomas Manton, *A Practical Commentary, or An Exposition with Notes on the Epistle of Jude* in *The Works of Thomas Manton: Volume 5* (Birmingham, AL: Solid Ground Christian Books, 2008).

Moo, *2 Peter and Jude*—Douglas J. Moo, *2 Peter and Jude*, The NIV Application Commentary (Grand Rapids, MI: Zondervan Publishing House, 1996).

Poole, *Jude—The Exegetical Labors of the Reverend Matthew Poole, Volume 79: 1 John–Jude*, trans. Steven Dilday, ed. April M. McLeod (Culpeper, VA: Master Poole Publishing, 2013).

WLC—Westminster Larger Catechism (1647)

Acknowledgements

I continue to thank God for my brothers and sisters at the Oceanside United Reformed Church, who have supported the ministry of the Word of God among the communities of North San Diego County for over sixteen years at the time of the writing of this book. You've had to listen to this donkey (Numbers 22) week in and week out for a long time. The fact that you come back for more is evidence that the Holy Spirit is still pouring out his grace among us! I marvel at your ability to listen and even more at your ability to live out the Word beyond my abilities to apply it to you. You encourage my heart to continue working on becoming a pastor whose duty and delight is to "preach the Word" (2 Timothy 4:2).

I thank a "true *father* in the faith" (1 Timothy 1:2), Dr. Hywel Jones, whose lectures through Jude's little letter sparked my interest to preach it twice throughout my ministry and who encouraged me to continue studying it so that I could write on it.

I thank my wife, Karajean, who continues to be my most honest and helpful sermon critic, telling me what I need to hear not what I want to hear: "She opens her mouth with wisdom, and the teaching of kindness is on her tongue" (Proverbs 31:26). I also thank my boys—Cyprian, Caiden, and Daxton—and my little girl—Sadie—who, without their knowing it, have made me a better communicator of the Word. "Out of *your* mouths *the Lord has* prepared praise" (Matthew 21:16).

Preface

THOSE who are content in knowing the Triune God of grace are called to contend in the name of the Triune God for that grace. Those who have been blessed with every spiritual blessing (Ephesians 1:3–14) are to fight against every spiritual force of evil (Ephesians 6:10–20). In the words of one hymn:

'Mid toil and tribulation
And tumult of her war,
She waits the consummation
Of peace forevermore.
Till with the vision glorious
Her longing eyes are blest,
And the great Church victorious
Shall be the Church at rest.[1]

Content yet contending. That's what I see as Jude's enduring message that is so relevant today. He begins with Christian contentment, locating believers' lives in the gospel of the Triune God. He calls us "called, beloved, kept" (v. 1). He prays for us to receive an abundance

---

1 From the hymn, "The Church's One Foundation," by Samuel J. Stone.

of "mercy, peace, and love" (v. 2). And while he planned to write to his original audience about the glories of this doctrine of salvation (v. 3), he was compelled to exhort them—and us—to enter a spiritual war and contend for the faith (vv. 3–23). The gospel causes in us a response. He then ends by reassuring us as those contending, that in Christ we can be content. While we fight, God keeps us and will present us before his throne in glory and with great joy (vv. 24–25).

And what a message this is for the church of Jesus Christ in our age in every corner of the earth. The enemies to fight are ever changing. But whether it was ancient Gnosticism, Arianism, or Pelagianism, medieval semi-Pelagianism, Sacramentalism, or the Inquisition, modern Rationalism, Liberalism, Communism, or now the Fascism of sexual identity politics and "human flourishing" apart from the Creator's will and boundaries, the Lord in whom God's people place their faith remains the same yesterday, today, and forever (Hebrews 13:8). Whether we are Christians in house churches in China, in the mountains of Pakistan, among the islands of Indonesia, or in "the West," we need to ever hold together the twin truths of what Jesus Christ has done for us in his life, death, and resurrection and what Jesus Christ is doing in us and through us by the ministry of his Holy Spirit (Galatians 3:13–14; Titus 2:11–14). As Christian preachers, we need to ever hold forth to our people this whole counsel of God (Acts 20:27) that we are at rest in the blessings that are ours in Jesus Christ while at the same time we are roused to battle by his Spirit for the glory of Christ's eternal kingdom. Speaking from my context as a Christian in the United States, we have so detached the Christian life from the universal kingdom of Christ that we have ended up focusing merely on the "done" aspects of Christ's work for us personally, leaving our churches at risk of becoming libertines. Or we have focused merely on the "do" aspects of our daily sanctification in Christ, leaving our churches at risk of becoming legalists.[2]

As a gospel minister, it is my solemn and joyful duty to proclaim a message of rest to restless sinners week in and week out (Matthew 11:28–30). It is also my duty to stir up God's children to holy activity for the glory of God, the edification of the church, and the extension of the kingdom in the salvation of the world (Philippians 2:12). This is the message that we preach and the message we pray is lived out in the world by our people.

In the context of the little letter of Jude, this means Christians are to know that they rest secure in the grip of the Triune God's grace. As Jesus said, no one can snatch us out of that grip (John 10:28–29). Christians are also to know that the walls of Zion are constantly under attack and that they are needed as soldiers on its walls (Isaiah 62:6–7).

That brings us to this book. The substance of this fresh exposition and application of Jude comes from two expository series I have done at the Oceanside United Reformed Church. Jude is one of those "go to" books for a sermon series because of its short length. And because of its interesting imagery it can even be preached multiple times over the course of a ministry, bringing out fresh applications every time. But Jude is so vital for our time for a more important reason: its urgent and timely message. The church in the first century faced enemies and opposition. And here we are as worldwide Christians facing down too many enemies to number in our time, whether philosophical or political. How did Jude respond? How are we to respond? What does

---

2 For an extremely helpful discussion on the relationship between antinomianism and legalism as "nonidentical twins that emerge from the same womb" of misunderstanding the nature of God, see Sinclair Ferguson, *The Whole Christ: Legalism, Antinomianism, & Gospel Assurance—Why the Marrow Controversy Still Matters* (Wheaton, IL: Crossway, 2016), 79–86.

this mean for how we evangelize, testify, and bear witness to the good news of Jesus Christ in such a world? Jude is an invaluable letter that equips us to do just that.

I pray the substance and the spirit of this book causes you to be content in your God's amazing grace as well as moves you to "contend for the faith once for all delivered to the saints" (Jude 3).

Daniel R. Hyde
Oceanside, California
June 2016

I
The Most Neglected Epistle

Jude 1–2

ON E of the blessings unknown to me before becoming a father was getting reacquainted with classic children's stories. One of my firstborn son's favorites was E. B. White's, *Charlotte's Web* (1952). Early on there is a scene where a farmer named Mr. Arable takes an axe out to the barn in the morning. His daughter, Fern, asks her mother why? The answer is that the night before a sow gave birth and there was a runt in the litter. Because the runt wouldn't be able to get enough nourishment and it would die of starvation, Mr. Arable was going to put the runt out of its misery before its misery started. Fern objected, took the runt for herself, and named it Wilbur. Just because it was small didn't mean it should be treated in such a way.

I wonder what is your attitude toward the small parts in the Word of God? Are they runts or treasures? If I were to ask you what was the most neglected book of the Old Testament, which book would you answer with? Perhaps a historical book, like the Chronicles? Or one of the obscure and small Minor Prophets, like Obadiah? Now if I turned that question to the New Testament, what would you say? Obviously we know the Gospels and Acts because they tell the story of Jesus' ministry while on earth and his continuing ministry from heaven by the Holy Spirit (Acts 1:1). We're familiar with the epistles of Paul, except perhaps for Philemon. We know about the majestic book of Hebrews, Peter's letters, John's letters, the practical James, and the heart-thrilling Revelation. But what have I left out? You may be thinking, "nothing," because, in fact, you're so unfamiliar with the book I've omitted. Tucked away at the end of our New Testament is a tiny letter of Jude—so tiny, in fact, that one preacher called it almost a postcard.[3] Jude has been called by at least one New Testament scholar, "the most neglected book in the New Testament."[4]

It's neglected, but necessary. Although Jude is probably the most neglected New Testament epistle, it is a part of the canon of Scripture, that is, the group of books that are the "ruler" (that's what "canon" means) of faith and life for Christians.[5] It was "breathed out by God" and is therefore "profitable for teaching, for reproof, for correction, and for training in righteousness" (2 Timothy 3:16). Jude is a part

---

3 Voddie Baucham, "Contending for the Faith." As found at http://www.sermonaudio. com/sermoninfo.asp?SID=5309038320.

4 D.J. Rowston, "The Most Neglected Book in the New Testament." *New Testament Studies* 21:4 (July 1975): 554–563.

5 For a brief description of the topic of the canon of Scripture, see Daniel R. Hyde, *Welcome to a Reformed Church: A Guide for Pilgrims* (2010; Orlando, FL: Reformation Trust, fourth printing 2015), 42–43. For more detailed information, see F. F. Bruce, *The Canon of Scripture* (Downers Grove, Ill.: InterVarsity Press, 1988), and, Herman N. Ridderbos, *Redemptive History and the New Testament Scriptures*, trans. H. De Jongste, rev. Richard B. Gaffin, Jr., Biblical & Theological Studies (1963; second rev. ed., Phillipsburg, N.J.: Presbyterian and Reformed, 1988).

of God's revelation. The church recognized this and received it as Scripture in such early documents as the second century *Muratorian Canon*.[6] Among the ancients who recognized Jude's inspiration was the early church theologian, Origen of Alexandria (185–254), who said Jude was "a letter of few lines, it is true, but filled with the healthful words of heavenly grace."[7]

Jude writes about this heavenly grace in this short yet highly organized and structured letter. Using the categories of classical Graeco-Roman rhetoric, we can see the following outline develop:

- The *introduction* (*exordium*) seeks to gain the audience's attention (vv. 1–2);

- The *narration* (*narratio*) seeks to inform the audience of the main argument (vv. 3–4);

- The *proofs* (*probatio*) seeks to develop the argument with evidence (vv. 5–16);

- The *conclusion* (*peroratio*) seeks the reader's emotional response (vv. 17–23);

- The *doxology* (*doxologia*) is an added element in Christian literature that gives glory to God (vv. 23–25).[8]

---

6 On this ancient document, see F. F. Bruce, *The Canon of Scripture* (Downers Grove, IL: InterVarsity Press, 1988), 158–169.

7 *Commentary on the Gospel According to Matthew*, 10.17, in *Ante-Nicene Fathers*, trans. John Patrick (1896; repr., Peabody, MA: Hendrickson Publishers, Inc., fourth printing 2004), 9:424.

8 For a detailed discussion of this rhetorical structure, see J. Daryl Charles, "Literary Artifice in the Epistle of Jude." *Zeitschrift für die Neutestamentliche Wissenschaft und die Kunde der Älteren Kirche* 82 (January 1, 1991): 106–124; Duane Frederick

Seeing Jude structured this way gives us an appreciation for *how* the Holy Spirit inspired Scripture. He did not dictate to Jude this letter in a mysterious "Holy Spirit Greek" that dropped out of heaven. Instead, the Holy Spirit spoke the Word of God and "carried along" Jude in the process like a ship "driven along" by the wind in its sail (2 Peter 1:21 cf. Acts 27:15).[9] He did this as Jude adapted a common form of writing in his day for a holy purpose. In other words, God uses the creativity of the humanity he created to communicate to us.[10]

Here I want to lead you in an exposition and application of Jude's attention grabbing introduction in verses 1–2. In this introduction, Jude grabs our attention with three of his twenty sets of literary triplets.

The Threefold Author

Jude—and therefore, the Holy Spirit—first grabs our attention with a threefold description of himself: "Jude," "servant," and "brother" (v. 1). So who is this "Jude?" This is our Anglicized version of his Greek name Judas (*Ioudas*), which in turn came from his Hebrew name Judah (*Yehudah*).

Several men in the New Testament are named *Ioudas*. This particular Jude has been understood by church fathers such as Clement of Alexandria (150–215) and Eusebius of Caesarea (260/265–339/340) to be one of the half-brothers of our Lord Jesus Christ (Matthew 13:55; Mark 6:3); therefore he is contrasted with Judas Iscariot, who denied our Lord.[11] He and his brother James were the half-brothers of Jesus

---

Watson, *Invention, Arrangement, and Style: Rhetorical Criticism of Jude and 2 Peter*, SBLDS 104 (Atlanta, GA: Scholar's Press, 1998). For a shorter discussion, see Gene L. Green, *Jude and 2 Peter*, Baker Exegetical Commentary on the New Testament (Grand Rapids: Baker Academic, 2008), 33–42.

9 These two passages used the same root verb *pherō*.

10 On this idea that "God loves matter," see C. S. Lewis, *Mere Christianity* (1952; reprinted, San Francisco, CA: Harper Collins, 2001), 63–64.

11 *James, 1–2 Peter, 1–3 John, Jude*, Ancient Christian Commentary on Scripture: New

being the sons of Joseph and Mary after Jesus "was conceived by the Holy Spirit; born of the Virgin Mary" (Apostles' Creed).[12]

As a close relative of the Lord who writes to a Christian audience, Jude is a picture of that "amazing grace" of which we sing "how sweet the sound."[13] How so? Recall the Gospel story when Jesus once returned to his hometown of Nazareth. There, Jesus' own friends and former neighbors rejected him. Worse yet was that the apostle John says, "For not even his brothers believed in him" (John 7:5). Jude, along with Jesus' family, even thought Jesus was "out of his mind" (Mark 3:21; cf. John 10:20). In Mark 3:20–35 there are two accounts of people making an accusation against Jesus. His family, who said he was "out of his mind,"[14] and the scribes who accused him of having "an unclean spirit" (Mark 3:30). In fact, the literary way these rejections are structured causes them to highlight one another. We read of his family in 3:20–21, and 3:31–35, and then sandwiched in between is the account of the scribes in 3:22–30.[15] His family thought he was crazy. Paul's later use of this term illustrates how serious Jesus' family's accusation was, when Paul contrasts being "beside ourselves"[16] (as his accusers said) with being "in our right mind" (2 Corinthians 5:13).

Jude is a picture to us of God's amazing grace because at one point in his life, Jude was just like you and me—an unbeliever. Yet here he is writing to the people of God as a *"servant* of Jesus Christ." He who

---

Testament, Volume XI, ed. Gerald L. Bray (Downers Grove, IL: InterVarsity Press, 2000), 245–246.

12 See Richard Bauckham, *Jude and the Relatives of Jesus in the Early Church* (Edinburgh: T. & T. Clark, 1990).

13 From the hymn, "Amazing Grace," by John Newton.

14 The Greek verb is *existēmi.*

15 On Mark 3, see William L. Lane, *The Gospel of Mark*, The New International Commentary on the New Testament (Grand Rapids, MI: William B. Eerdmans Publishing Company, 1974), 137–139.

16 The Greek verb is the same as in Mark 3:21: *existēmi.*

once scoffed at Jesus now served Jesus. He who once slandered Jesus now was Jesus' slave (*doulos*). The only reason he changed his attitude about Jesus was that he *was* changed—by the Lord. As Paul said of himself once, in contrast to his former life of persecuting Christians: "by the grace of God I am what I am" (1 Corinthians 15:10). God's grace in the life of sinners is "delightful, astonishing, mysterious, and ineffable" (CD 3/4.12).

Jude was now Jesus' slave. This means that just like the prophets of old he was called and commissioned to speak on behalf of the Lord (Isaiah 6). And just like you and me, he was also a servant who belonged to the Jesus "with body and soul, both in life and in death" (HC, Q&A 1). What a lesson this is for us as pastors. In the words of C. H. Spurgeon, "when we speak as ministers, and not as men; as preachers, instead of penitents; as theologians instead of disciples, we fail."[17] In calling himself the Lord's "servant," he was following the example of Jesus' own mother, who also called herself by the title "servant of the Lord" (Luke 1:38). As such a servant, Jude encourages those of us who are pastors to remember that we are just that, servants, who must give an account to the Master one day (Hebrews 13:17). On the other hand, this means that God's people must regard their pastors as servants *of the Lord* (1 Corinthians 4:1). This is a high honor: "The apostles generally urge it as one of the fairest flowers in their garland, the honour of being Christ's servants; yea, Christ himself counteth it no dishonor to be styled God's servant."[18]

And as a prophetic servant of the Lord we can sense his urgency. Notice that he originally intended to write about their "common salvation" (v. 3), as he had come to believe in Jesus as the Messiah

---

17 C.H. Spurgeon, *An All-Round Ministry* (1900; reprinted, Edinburgh: The Banner of Truth Trust, 1986), 64.

18 Manton, *Jude*, 5:11.

and Savior as well. But as one who had been "snatch[ed] ... out of the fire" (v. 23) he instead sought to rouse believers by sounding the wake-up alarm "to contend for the faith" because some had infiltrated the church and turned "the grace of our God into sensuality" (vv. 3, 4). He also urgently exhorted the church to "build yourselves up in your most holy faith" (v. 20). This urgency is seen in Jude's continual use of the personal pronouns "you/your/our" (vv. 2, 3, 4, 5, 12, 17, 18, 20, 21, 24, 25) in contrast to the false teachers whom he impersonally calls "these/those" (vv. 7, 8, 10, 12, 14, 16, 19).

This urgent wake-up alarm is for us. Jude writes to no specific church or group of churches, but a truly "catholic epistle," meaning that his letter was meant for all believers in all times and in all places. Therefore this transformed unbeliever writes to us who are gathered into Christ's church some two thousand years later. He urgently writes to all of us, whether we are pastors, elders, or members, to be aware that within the church are some who have come to use the grace of God as an opportunity to live any way they please. In the Reformation period these people were called the "Libertines," as they flaunted their liberty; in our day we call these antinomians, that is, those who are against the law of God.[19] Jude, who once lived in unbelief but was powerfully changed knows the power of the grace of God that causes us to live thankful lives, unlike "these" people whose desires were for sexual pleasure (vv. 4, 7, 16), power pleasure (vv. 8, 16), and personal pleasure (v. 12).

---

19 For an excellent survey of the history of antinomianism and its contemporary application, see Mark Jones, *Antinomianism: Reformed Theology's Unwelcome Guest?* (Phillipsburg: P&R Publishing, 2013).

The Threefold Recipients

Jude goes on to grab our attention with a threefold repetition about his audience. He describes us as "called," "beloved," and "kept" (v. 1). These are the fruits of God's electing grace (Romans 8:29).[20]

This description of his recipients in the Greek text illuminates the meaning of what Jude is saying. Jude here uses what is called an *inclusio*, that is, he includes a sentence in between two other words at the beginning and end. Our English text begins, "To those who are called," and then continues with the rest of the sentence. In the Greek text this phrase is only two words (*tois kletois*). What Jude does is to separate these two words and place the rest of the sentence in between them; hence, the *inclusio*. He says, "*To those* ... beloved in God the Father and kept for Jesus Christ ... *who are called*." What Jude is saying is that it is those who are called by God that are the ones who are loved by God and preserved by Jesus Christ. It is those who are called in time that have already been loved from eternity past and that will be preserved for Jesus Christ unto eternity future (Romans 8:30; 1 Peter 1:3–5). If Romans 8:29–30 has been called "the golden chain of salvation," then Jude 1 is the silver chain. What we notice in these titles is the super-abounding grace upon grace of God towards sinners like Jude, me, and you (Romans 5:20; John 1:16).

You are "called" by God, literally, "the called." The Scriptures use this term in two senses: either outward or inward, either external or internal, or either general or effectual. Remember Jesus' words: "For many are called, but few are chosen" (Matthew 22:14). Many are called to believe the gospel outwardly, externally, and generally. But here Jude is speaking of that inward, internal, and effectual call of the gospel by which the Holy Spirit irresistibly regenerates us and converts us.[21]

---

20 Calvin, *Commentary*, 322; Calvin, *Exposition*, 6.
21 Poole, *Jude*, 224–225.

This is what Paul meant when he said, "Those whom he predestined he also called" (Romans 8:30). As the ancient preacher Oecumenius (*ca.* 600) said, "he refers to his correspondents as those who have been 'called,' because it was not they who decided to follow Jesus, but God who reached out to call them to his service."[22] I couldn't say it any better as a Reformed preacher!

To be the called of God means to be "called to belong to Jesus Christ" (Romans 1:6). We are called from self to the Savior. In 1 Corinthians 1:18 and following the apostle Paul speaks of the preaching of Christ crucified as foolishness and a stumbling block to Greeks and Jews, but then says, "but to those who are called," Christ is the wisdom and power of God. We are called from our misery in sin to joy and happiness in the Savior as those who "proclaim the excellencies of him who called [us] out of darkness into his marvelous light" (1 Peter 2:9). For us who believe in Jesus Christ our eyes which were once blind have been given sight; our souls which were once dead have been given life.

And notice that Jude not only says that we have been effectually called to faith and life in Jesus Christ in space, time, and history, for we who are called are the very same ones whom God the Father has loved from all eternity. We are "beloved in God the Father."[23] Jude here uses the perfect tense and the passive voice for this verb. The

---

22 *James, 1–2 Peter, 1–3 John, Jude*, ed. Bray, 246.

23 John Calvin called this reading a "corruption." Calvin, *Commentary*, 323. The King James Version and New King James Version has "sanctified" here instead of "beloved." The reading "sanctified" is based on the Majority Text and P. The reading "beloved" is supported by older and better manuscripts, such as, p72 (3rd/4th c.), Codex Sinaiticus (4th c.), Codex Alexandrinus (5th c.), and Codex Bezae (4th c.). Bruce Metzger says that the reading "sanctified" "was introduced by copyists in order to avoid the difficult and unusual combination" of "beloved in God the Father," *A Textual Commentary on the Greek New Testament* (corrected edition; London: United Bible Societies, 1975), 723.

force of this syntactical choice of word can rendered, "those who have been loved." The perfect tense of this verb signifies a past action with ongoing results in the present, and in this case, in the future: "Who shall separate us from the love of Christ? ... For I am sure that neither death nor life, nor angels nor rulers, nor things present nor things to come, nor powers, nor height nor depth, nor anything else in all creation, will be able to separate us from the love of God in Christ Jesus our Lord" (Romans 8:35, 38–39). We who were beloved in God the Father's bosom from all eternity, were loved when he called us to Christ, and will continue to be loved by him unto eternity future. The passive voice of this verb gives the force that we are being loved, that we are the recipients and the objects of God's love from outside of us. "In this is love, not that we have loved God but that he loved us and sent his Son to be the propitiation for our sins" (1 John 4:10). And to be loved "in God the Father"[24] speaks of the tenderness and intimacy of this love. As one commentator said, "His love enfolds them."[25] We experience as adopted sons of God the Father that love which the eternal Son has ever known "in the bosom of the Father" (John 1:18; NASB). As Thomas Manton (1620–1677) said, "Nothing maketh the saints love God more than the unchangeableness of his love."[26]

Jude ends this triad to his recipients saying we are "kept for Jesus Christ." Again, the verb "kept" is a perfect passive. The one doing the keeping is the Father, the ones being kept are the called, and the one

---

24 On the interpretive issue of the Greek preposition *en* being "beloved *in* God" or "beloved *by* God," see Moo, *2 Peter and Jude*, 223; Thomas R. Schreiner *1, 2 Peter, Jude*, The New American Commentary: Volume 37 (Nashville, TN: Broadman & Holman Publishers, 2003), 430.

25 J.N.D. Kelly, *A Commentary on the Epistles of Peter and of Jude* (New York: Harper & Row, 1969), 243.

26 Manton, *Jude*, 5:49.

receiving those kept is Jesus Christ. Thomas Manton said, "Jesus Christ is the cabinet wherein God's jewels are kept."[27] We are his jewels.

We are kept "for"[28] Jesus Christ, as our English Standard Version says, which means that we are kept unto the Day in which Christ returns to take us to himself in glory (1 Thessalonians 5:23). The mystery of the relationship between the preservation of the saints and the perseverance of the saints is seen when our text is compared with verse 21, which says, "Keep yourselves in the love of God, waiting for the mercy of our Lord Jesus Christ that leads to eternal life." The verb "to keep" is used in many contexts in the New Testament. It can be used in the sense "keep watch over, guard" (of a prisoner or building); "hold, reserve, preserve for a purpose or for a time" (1 Peter 1:4–5; 1 Thessalonians 5:23; 2 Peter 2:4, 9, 17, 3:7); to be "preserved unharmed, undisturbed" (Jude 21); to keep in the sense "do not lose" (1 Timothy 4:7; Jude 6); and "to protect" (John 17:15). We who are kept by God's love are to keep on loving him.

As a member of the people of God, you are so privileged in having these titles upon your head—"called," "beloved," "kept"—just as they were used in the Old Testament of Israel, the Lord's called (Isaiah 41:19; 42:6; 48:12, 15; 49:1; 54:6), beloved (Deuteronomy 32:15; 33:5, 26; 2 Chronicles 20:7; Psalm 28:6; Isaiah 5:1; 42:1; 43:4; 44:2), and kept people (Isaiah 42:6; 49:8).

John Calvin (1509–1564) summed this verse up when he said, "there is a threefold blessing of God upon all men of religion: He calls them

---

27 Manton, *Jude*, 5:43.
28 This is the translation of the ESV and NASB. The NIV puts this translation in a footnote. On the interpretive issues of the Greek dative case, see Moo, *2 Peter and Jude*, 223; Schreiner *1, 2 Peter, Jude*, 430–431.

to share in the Gospel, He re-creates them by His Spirit unto newness of life, and by Christ's arm, He defends them."[29]

The Threefold Prayer

Jude's final threefold repetition to grab our attention is a threefold prayer. He also does this by using the rare optative mood in verse 2, which expresses his deep desire and emotion in the form of a prayer: "O may the mercy, peace, and love of this calling, loving, and keeping God overflow to you!"

As a former enemy of his very own brother, Jude prays that we who deserve misery would experience the mercy of God—the experience of not getting what we deserve but of receiving God's lavishness. We deserve everlasting wrath and condemnation because of our sins, but God's wrath has been averted by placing it upon his very own Son, our Lord Jesus Christ. The Belgic Confession so beautifully expresses this when it says, "God therefore manifested His justice against His Son when He laid our iniquities upon Him, and poured forth His mercy and goodness on us, who were guilty and worthy of damnation, out of mere and perfect love ..." (BC, article 20). Beloved of God: receive his mercy.

Jude also desires that we experience the peace of God. It is because we are in the status of no longer being the enemies of God (Romans 5:10), but the recipients of his mercy that we have the experience of peace: "Since we have been justified by faith, we have peace with God through our Lord Jesus Christ" (Romans 5:1). In worldly terms, we think of peace as the absence of war, even as we speak of "peace time." But peace is not only the absence of enmity but it is the positive and blessed state of friendship. It's not the photo-op peace we see in the

---

29 Calvin, *Commentary*, 323.

news when two nations' leaders shake hands and smile for the camera. It is real. Friends of God: receive his peace.

Jude closes his prayer to God that we would experience the love of God—that infinite and gracious self-giving of God to us. This is that active giving on God's part to us in which "he gave his only Son" (John 3:16). This is that demonstration of God in that "while we were still sinners, Christ died for us" (Romans 5:8). Manton said it like this: "God loveth the lowest saint more than the highest angel loveth God ... the more sense we have of the love of God, the stronger is our love to him."[30] People of God: receive his love.

Neglected, but so beneficial, Jude's little epistle begins with his prayer that you would deeply and intensely feel the Lord "multiply" or fill you with these blessings and benefits upon you day after day until our Savior returns. Jude's letter is no unnecessary runt in the canon of the New Testament. It offers to us "the riches of [Christ's] glory" (Ephesians 3:16) in the gospel that brings us such contentment in the midst of the conflict in which we are to contend.

---

30 Manton, *Jude*, 5:73.

2
Contend for the Faith

Jude 3–4

❧ ❦

In his play, *The Life of King Henry V*, William Shakespeare (1564–1616) told the story of the English king's speech before the Battle of Agincourt on October 25, 1415 (Act 4, Scene 3). Facing a well-rested army with five to one supremacy, morale was virtually non-existent. As Salisbury said, "God's arm strike with us! 'tis a fearful odds." And when Westmoreland opined, "O that we now had here but one ten thousand of those men in England that do no work to-day!," King Henry gave his famous Saint Crispin's Day speech to rouse his troops:

> … This story shall the good man teach his son;
> And Crispin Crispian shall ne'er go by,
> From this day to the ending of the world,
> But we in it shall be remember'd;
> We few, we happy few, we band of brothers;

For he to-day that sheds his blood with me
Shall be my brother; be he ne'er so vile,
This day shall gentle his condition:
And gentlemen in England now a-bed
Shall think themselves accursed they were not here,
And hold their manhoods cheap whiles any speaks
That fought with us upon Saint Crispin's day.

The rest, as they say, is history. Such a heart-pumping appeal to spiritual war is what we find in the letter of Jude. The author passionately wrote to ancient Christians to embolden them as armies of the Lord for battle despite the odds. And, I might add, the very act of letter writing shows Jude's passionate care about these people because he took the time to write, incurred the expense of writing, and underwent the effort to have the letter delivered, all to communicate his message. For example, E. Randolph Richards has estimated the cost and time involved in the writing of Paul's letters. His longest, Romans, may have taken 11.5 hours to write (2–3 days for a copy) and cost $2,900 in today's money, while his shortest letter comparable to Jude was Philemon, which may have taken half an hour to write and $130.[31]

And by the Holy Spirit's ministry this letter rouses us. The church on earth in this age is what theologians have called "the church militant," because it is called to put on armor (Ephesians 6:10–20) and fight the good spiritual battle of faith (1 Timothy 6:12; 2 Timothy 4:7). The people of God have always been under attack since the serpent entered the Garden (Genesis 3), are under attack now, and always will be under attack both from without and from within until the Lord returns.

31 See E. Randolph Richards, *Paul and First-Century Letter Writing: Secretaries, Composition and Collection* (Downers Grove, IL: IVP Academic, 2004), 161–169.

Jude not only calls us to prepare for battle, but he also gives us the battle plan as he details our enemy as well as our methods of attack.

One of the hardest realities we have to learn in this life is that our warfare is not geo-political, but theological and spiritual. In the history of Christianity's interaction with civilizations and cultures, this hasn't always been understood. But recall the words of Paul, who said, "For though we walk in the flesh, we are not waging war according to the flesh. For the weapons of our warfare are not of the flesh but have divine power to destroy strongholds. We destroy arguments and every lofty opinion raised against the knowledge of God, and take every thought captive to obey Christ" (2 Corinthians 10:3–5). He said this again in his famous "armor of God" passage: "For we do not wrestle against flesh and blood, but against the rulers, against the authorities, against the cosmic powers over this present darkness, against the spiritual forces of evil in the heavenly places" (Ephesians 6:12).

After introducing himself, addressing us, and praying for us, Jude goes on in verses 3–4 with his narration[32] that tells his audience what his main argument is. This is not merely informational but inspirational, exhorting us to contend for the faith.

The Urgency of Contending

"The price of peace is eternal vigilance." This oft-quoted phrase and others related to it communicate the idea that we must ever be on guard. And as Jude exhorts us to contend for the faith, this contention is urgent. He addresses his "beloved" (v. 3; *agapētoi*), whom he said were "beloved (*ēgapēmenois*) in [or, by] God the Father" (v. 1) and for whom he prayed would receive the multiplication of God's "love" (v. 2; *agapē*). And he acknowledges to these brothers and sisters that he originally was "very eager to write to you about our common

---

32 See above p.17 for outline.

salvation." In calling it a "common salvation" he shows them that he was a "practising instructor."[33] He was "very eager" to encourage them in their salvation. We can feel his deep and intense passion for them to rejoice in the glorious truths of the gospel with questions like who saves, who are saved, how they are saved, from what they are saved, and why they are saved? This salvation should be the heartbeat of every pastor and all his people.

But while Jude eagerly desired to write about that salvation about which nothing better can be written about, the Holy Spirit knew the church needed to hear something more urgently.[34] He says, "I found it necessary to write appealing to you to contend for the faith that was once for all delivered to the saints" (v. 3). This reminds us that "no prophecy was ever produced by the will of man;" instead, "they were carried along by the Holy Spirit" (2 Peter 1:21). This is such an important lesson for us to grasp. The Word of God is what God says we need, not what we think we need. It's what God wants for us, not what we want for ourselves. And as pastors we need to know our people's deepest needs and be able to speak from God to them.

Jude's urgency is seen in his use of the term "contend" (*epagōnizesthai*). The word he uses comes into our English language as "agonize." What is Jude saying? Look with me elsewhere in the New Testament. This verb is used in athletic and military contexts. In 1 Corinthians 9:24–25 Paul says, "Do you not know that in a race all the runners run, but only one receives the prize. So run that you may obtain it. Every *athlete* exercises self-control in all things. They do it to receive a perishable wreath, but we an imperishable." The English Standard Version translation of "athlete" makes a verb a noun. The verb speaks

---

33 Calvin, *Commentary*, 324.

34 Hywel Jones, "The Value of an Unwritten Letter (Part 1)." *The Outlook* 50:11 (December 2000): 5.

of one who competes (NASB; NIV) or strives (KJV). It's the verb used by Jude in verse 3. The Christian is an agonizer, contending for victory. Think of images or live shots you've seen of runners' faces as they race against their competitors. Can you see that image in your mind? How hard are they straining for the goal? In Colossians 1:29 Paul describes his ministry to "present everyone mature in Christ" (Colossians 1:28), saying, "For this I toil, *struggling* with all his energy." Again, in 1 Timothy 4:10 Paul contrasts bodily exercise with godliness, which leads to life in the world to come. Then he says, "To this end [eternal life] we toil and *strive*." It's also used with military imagery. In 1 Timothy 6:12 Paul famously says, "*Fight* the good *fight* of faith," and in his last letter, "I have *fought* the good *fight*" (2 Timothy 4:7). In Ephesians 6:12 Paul speaks of hand-to-hand combat: "For we do not *wrestle* against flesh and blood." John Calvin said this verse was an exhortation: "you must apply yourselves to studying and employing all your strength to be confirmed in the faith."[35]

Those Doing the Contending

This brings up a practical point in our text. Who is to "contend?" It's urgent for there to be agonizing, contending, and fighting for the faith, but by whom?

First, let me mention ministers. One might think of ancient church fathers we call "the apologists"—men like Justin Martyr (100–165). One might think of those whom early Reformation churches called "the doctors of the church." And there are many modern examples of great men who preach, teach, and write to defend the faith. And of course this is a calling of all ministers of the Word, as Paul exhorted Timothy and Titus (2 Timothy 2:2; Titus 1:9). But we cannot be tempted to think this urgency is their responsibility alone, as we will see below.

---

35 "Calvin, *Exposition*, 7.

Second, and most importantly for our text is to notice whom Jude is addressing. "*Beloved*, although I was very eager to write to *you* about *our* common salvation, I found it necessary to write appealing to *you* to contend for the faith." And this "faith … was once for all delivered to the *saints*."

It is the duty of all the members of the body of Christ to contend for the faith. It's not merely for the theologians, the pastors, or the elders. We are all to be urgently alert and awake. This means *you* are to know what you believe and why you believe it so that you can engage the spiritual war for truth. As Peter told his hearers: "but in your hearts honor Christ the Lord as holy, always being prepared to make a defense to anyone who asks you for a reason for the hope that is in you; yet do it with gentleness and respect" (1 Peter 3:15).

One thing that is helpful to remember in this is that just as in an army there are many different roles, so too in our spiritual warfare there are many roles for us all to play. Some are strategists and some are soldiers. Some are communications experts and some are logistics experts. Some are on the front lines and some are behind the scenes, while even some are behind enemy lines. We all have a role to play. What is yours?

The Object of Contending

The next question is for what are we contending? We can be urgently alert and awake all we want, but we have to be so for something. Zeal without knowledge is misspent. And so Jude writes to us to contend for "the faith that was once for all delivered to the saints." Notice that "the faith" is objective, not subjective. It is not faith in general for which we are to contend, but *the* faith, the *what* of what we believe (cf. 1 Timothy 4:1). Elsewhere this is called "the apostles' doctrine" (Acts 2:42), "the gospel" (e.g., 1 Corinthians 15:1), "the faith" (Philippians 1:27; Colossians 2:6–7), "the truth" (Colossians 1:5), "the words of the faith of the good doctrine" (1 Timothy 4:6), the "form of teaching" (Romans 6:17; NASB), "the pattern of the sounds words" (2 Timothy 1:13), "sound teaching" (2 Timothy 4:3; Titus 1:9) and "the teaching" (2 John 9). And this faith for which we are to fight was "once for all delivered to the saints." The word for "delivered" is translated elsewhere in the New Testament as "the tradition" (1 Corinthians 15:1–8; 2 Thessalonians 3:6; 1 Timothy 1:10; 6:3; 2 Timothy 1:13; 4:3; Titus 1:9; 2:1). Luke uses it to speak of the "narrative of the things that have been accomplished among us" as passed down by "ministers of the word" (Luke 1:2). Paul speaks of the creedal-like statement of Christ's death, burial, and resurrection as something passed down (1 Corinthians 15:3). The faith which Jude exhorts us to fight for are those basic, rudimentary truths that the Holy Spirit led the apostles to remembrance of (John 14:26), that they passed down to the next generation, especially to pastors (1 Timothy 1:10; 2 Timothy 1:3, 4:3; Titus 1:9, 21, 2:14), and that have reached us in the sacred Scriptures. This is why Thomas Manton said this word speaks of the things "delivered to our custody that we may keep it for posterity."[36] The faith is not changing. It is not new. This is instructive for us against both the Pope and Pentecostalism. The church cannot determine new articles of faith. And the Holy Spirit is not communicating new truth today. He has spoken.

It is our duty to proclaim, propagate, and publish the Word of God as far and as wide as humanly possible in this life. It is also our duty to preserve and protect it from error so that the next generation has something to proclaim.

This means that we contend urgently because the Christian Faith is something worth fighting for. "Buy the truth and sell it not. It is a

---

36 Manton, *Jude*, 5:104.

commodity that should be bought at any rate, but sold by no means
… Christ thought it worth his blood to purchase the gospel."[37] It is
the truth that Jesus promised his disciples the Holy Spirit would lead
them in (John 16:13). And now it's passed down. Are we willing to
die for our faith as Jude's brother James did?[38] Are we willing to be
crucified upside down as Peter was? This is why it is so necessary for
us to know what we believe, why we believe it, and how to use what
we believe when we are asked why we believe! We live in an age of
doctrinal laziness and indifference. We must not become weary of
this faith as the church in Ephesus did (Revelation 2:1–7), but must
always be urgently on the offensive. As one hymn says,

> Faith of our fathers! we will strive
> to win all nations unto thee,
> and through the truth that comes from God,
> the world shall then be truly free:
> faith of our fathers, holy faith!
> We will be true to thee till death!
>
> Faith of our fathers! we will love
> both friend and foe in all our strife;
> and preach thee, too, as love knows how,
> by kindly words and virtuous life:
> faith of our fathers, holy faith!
> We will be true to thee till death![39]

Yet in our contending we are not to be contentious. We are to
speak the truth, but to do so in love (Ephesians 4:15). We are to
preserve the garden of God's truth without plowing over the people
trampling through it. We are enabled to do this by turning our hearts

---

37 Manton, *Jude*, 5:115.
38 Josephus, *Antiquities*, 20.9.1.
39 From the hymn, "Faith of Our Fathers," by Frederick William Faber.

and minds to the Word of God. As the ancient pastor and martyr, Polycarp (69–155), said, "let us abandon the vanities of the crowd and their false teachings; let us return to the word which was delivered to us from the beginning."[40]

The Necessity for Contending

Remember that Jude said "I found it *necessary* to write appealing to you" (v. 3). Why was it necessary? The little word "for" connects the urgency of verse 3 with the necessity of verse 4: "For certain people have crept in unnoticed who long ago were designated for this condemnation, ungodly people, who pervert the grace of our God into sensuality and deny our only Master and Lord, Jesus Christ."

Who were these people whom the church needed to contend against? Jude doesn't even name them. They are just "certain people." To withhold someone's name is to hold them in contempt. I once dealt with an inter-personal struggle between two believers in which one would always refer to the other as "the woman" or "my malefactor." It was a way of showing moral superiority. In that case it was unjustified. In Jude's case it was warranted because of what these "certain people" were doing and seeking to lead other to do.[41]

And notice the method of these people: they "have crept in unnoticed." This is the only time this verb is used in the Word of God. It's no coincidence that Jude likens these people to serpents. They were like the serpent in the Garden, who snuck past the boundary

---

40 "The Letter of St. Polycarp to the Philippians," ch. 7, trans. Francis X. Glimm, The Fathers of the Church (New York, NY: Cima Publishing Co., Inc., 1947), 139.

41 This is also evidence that Jude used *epideictic discourse*, which was a rhetorical strategy to praise an audience (*laudatio*) as well as place blame on another (*vituperatio*). Stephan J. Joubert, "Persuasion in the Letter of Jude." *The Journal for the Study of the New Testament* 58 (1995): 75–87.

of the Garden,[42] which Adam was to guard,[43] only to appear before Eve. They were like wolves in sheep's clothing (Matthew 7:15). They were like the enemies of God who in the days when the temple was being rebuilt, said, "Let us build with you, for we worship your God as you do" (Ezra 4:2). They were like the "false brothers" in Galatia "secretly brought in—who slipped in to spy out our freedom that we have in Christ Jesus" (Galatians 2:4). They were like those "false prophets" of old and those "false teachers" of the first century "who will secretly bring in destructive heresies" (2 Peter 2:1). They were like those plausible sounding teachers of Ephesus, whose "human cunning" and "craftiness in deceitful schemes" caused the church to be like "children, tossed to and fro by the waves and carried about by every wind of doctrine" (Ephesians 4:14). They had a profession of faith, but only for ulterior motives; they came in under a guise; only to unveil their masks and reveal their true colors later. As Thomas Manton described them, they are "like worms bred within the body, sought to devour the entrails and eat out the very bowels of it."[44]

And so Jude also calls them "ungodly (*asebeis*) people." He says, literally, that they are not worshippers of God (Romans 4:5; 5:6; 1 Timothy 1:9; 1 Peter 4:18; 2 Peter 2:5–6; 3:7). They were not philosophical atheists, but practical atheists, even though they claimed to believe in God they lived like he had no authority over them. In 2 Peter 2 those who died in the Flood and at Sodom and Gomorrah are described as being "ungodly" (2 Peter 2:5–6) and in 2 Peter 3 those who scoff at the coming of Christ are called "ungodly" (2 Peter 3:7).

---

42 David H. Wheaton, "Jude," in *The New Bible Commentary: Revised*, ed. D. Guthrie and J.A. Motyer (Grand Rapids: Eerdmans, 1970), 1275.

43 Meredith G. Kline, *Kingdom Prologue: Genesis Foundations for a Covenantal Worldview* (Overland Park, KS: Two Age Press, 2000), 85–87. This book may be found at www.twoagepress.org.

44 Manton, *Jude*, 5:6

False doctrines from false teachers are not mere theological problems: they are moral.

He then defines what these ungodly people were saying and doing. They "pervert the grace of our God into sensuality" (Jude 4). In a word, they had an over-realized eschatology in terms of the experience of salvation.[45] The New Testament mentions many different strategies of false teachers. Sometimes they came with a message of greater strictness than that which God required (Colossians 2:18). Sometimes they came with a message of a higher gospel, which Paul called "another gospel" (Galatians 1:3) and "another Jesus" (2 Corinthians 11:4). Sometimes they came with a message of a greater, deeper learning (1 Timothy 6:20). Here, though, it was a message of license. As William Cowper (1731–1800) wrote:

Too many, Lord, abuse Thy grace,
In this licentious day;
And while they boast they see Thy face,
They turn their own away.

The pardon, such presume upon,
They do not beg, but steal;
And when they plead it at Thy throne,
Oh! where's the Spirit's seal?

Was it for this, ye lawless tribe,
The dear Redeemer bled?
Is this the grace the saints imbibe
From Christ the living Head?

---

45 Ralph P. Martin, "Jude," in Andrew Chester and Ralph P. Martin, *The Theology of the Letters of James, Peter, and Jude*, New Testament Theology (1994; repr., Cambridge: Cambridge University Press, 1996), 72–75.

Ah, Lord, we know Thy chosen few
Are fed with heavenly fare;
But these, the wretched husks they chew
Proclaim them what they are.

The liberty our hearts implore
Is not to live in sin;
But still to wait at wisdom's door,
Till mercy calls us in.[46]

If we do not contend for the faith there will be no more faith. If we do not contend for the faith there will be no grace from God. If we do not contend for the faith all we will have remaining is us, in our sins.

Bede (672–735) used the illustration of the coming of our Lord softening the hard edges of the law of God, such as stoning for various transgressions. Now he allows repentance as a means of receiving forgiveness. Yet these relax the law even more and say there is no punishment at all.[47] "They prostituted themselves and others to a foul and blasphemous career of sin."[48] Notice the examples he goes on to give: Sodom and Gomorrah's sexual immorality (Jude 7). He says these people "defile the flesh" (Jude 8) and follow "their own sinful desires" (Jude 16). In a word, they turned the liberty we have from the guilt and punishment of our sins by God's grace into a license to sin.[49] The word for "sensuality" often means sexual sin in the New Testament (Romans 13:13; 2 Corinthians 12:21; Galatians 5:19). This is what some slanderously said of the apostles so that Paul (Romans 6; Galatians 5:13) and Peter (1 Peter 2:16; 2 Peter 2:19) had to respond saying that the gospel's liberty does not lead to license. This is what some in the

---

46 From the hymn, "Too Many, Lord, Abuse Thy Grace," by William Cowper.
47 *James, 1–2 Peter, 1–3 John, Jude,* ed. Bray, 250.
48 Calvin, *Commentary,* 325.
49 In the Reformation these were called the "libertines." See Calvin, *Jude,* 433.

past said about the Reformed doctrine of God's preserving grace of his children throughout their lives. According to them it is "an opiate of the flesh […] harmful to godliness, good morals, prayer, and other holy exercises" (CD 5, Rejection of Errors 6). They argued from God's mercy into license, which John Trapp (1601–1669) called "the devil's logic."[50] These people turn grace into a "get out of jail free card."

Jude was so urgent because of their motives. The effect of what we read is that they were saying something like, "Your orthodox ministers are hampering your Christian freedom with their exactness, their call to deny your God-given nature, their call to mortify your pleasures and desires."[51] As Peter said, "They promise liberty, and allure through the lusts of the flesh" (2 Peter 2:18).

By doing this, they "deny our only Lord and Master, Jesus Christ."[52] They do not deny the Lord with their lips, for that would be too obvious, but they deny him with their lives.[53] Jude brings this out by using two titles to describe Jesus. The English "Master" is the ordinary Greek word for Jesus being called "Lord"—*kurios*. But Jude adds another title, which our English so weakly translates as "Lord." Jude calls him *despotēs*, that is, one who is the Sovereign, the Ruler of a people.[54] It comes into English as a Despot. He is the sole ruler, not you or I.

The application was clear: "May those who are called Christians

---

50 John Trapp, *A Commentary or Exposition Upon All the Epistles and the Revelation of John the Divine* (London, 1647), 489.

51 Manton, *Jude*, 5:104.

52 Both apply to Jesus, as the single definite article "the" in Greek governs both nouns. On the interpretive issues, see Moo, *2 Peter and Jude*, 230–231.

53 Didymus the Blind, in *James, 1–2 Peter, 1–3 John, Jude*, ed. Bray, 249; Luther, *Sermons*, 204–205.

54 It is used of the Father exclusively in the New Testament (e.g., Luke 2:29; 2 Tim 2:21; Acts 4:24; Revelation 6:10), except in 2 Peter 2:1 and here in Jude 4, where it is used of Christ.

and under this name 'pervert the grace of God into licentiousness' beware, lest they share the fate of those people!"[55]

And like all of these enemies, Jude's foes were "long ago … designated for this condemnation." The Holy Spirit had already[56] written about their condemnation before in the Old Testament[57] as well as in "the predictions of the apostles of our Lord Jesus Christ" (Jude 17).

Conclusion

Jude is a difficult book. It doesn't tickle our ears. It doesn't build self-esteem. But it has a negative theme to it: the church is under attack! It is written to show how to fight for the faith in the place where the faith shouldn't have to be fought for: the church. It rouses us as the army of the Lord in our day when people are fond of saying, "Let's all just get along" and "Doctrine divides, love unites." Fight, for there is something worth fighting for.

---

55 Luther, *Sermons*, 205.

56 The Greek word translated "long ago" in the ESV is *palai*, which may be translated "already" (cf. Mark 15:44). This is the view of Christopher Green, *The Message of 2 Peter & Jude* (The Bible Speaks Today; Downers Grove: IVP, 1995), 177; Moo, *2 Peter & Jude*, 230; Michael Green, *The Second Epistle General of Peter and the General Epistle of Jude* (Tyndale New Testament Commentaries; Grand Rapids: Eerdmans, 1968), 160; Richard J. Bauckham, *Jude, 2 Peter* (Word Biblical Commentary; Waco: Word, 1983), 35–36.

57 This phrase can also be understood in the sense of foreordination to reprobation. This is how early church fathers Clement of Alexandria (153–217) and Andreas (*ca.* seventh c.) interpreted the phrase in Clement of Alexandria, "Comments on the Epistle of Jude," in *Ante-Nicene Fathers*, trans. William Wilson, 10 vols. (1885; repr., Peabody, MA: Hendrickson Publishers, Inc., fourth printing 2004), 2:573 col. 2, and, *James, 1–2 Peter, 1–3 John, Jude*, ed. Bray, 249–250. As well, among commentators and theologians this is the view of Calvin, *Commentary*, 325; *Exposition*, 7; Manton, *Jude*, 5:125, 128–133; Poole, *Jude*, 227–229; Simon J. Kistemaker, *Exposition of the Epistles of Peter and of the Epistle of Jude*, New Testament Commentary (1987; Grand Rapids, MI: Baker Book House, second printing 1988), 374; Wayne Grudem, *Systematic Theology* (Grand Rapids: Zondervan, 1994), 703.

Jude is such a needed and relevant book for our time, as it has been in times past. In the Reformation period, we see that Jude was seen to be almost transparent to the culture surrounding the Reformers. Of Jude, Martin Luther said, "It is nothing more than an epistle directed against our clerics—bishops, priests, and monks."[58] Calvin says of Jude

> Now, if we consider what Satan has attempted in our age, from the commencement of the revived gospel, and what arts he still busily employs to subvert the faith, and the fear of God, what was a useful warning in the time of Jude, is more than necessary in our age.[59]

We need to study to show ourselves approved, pray for God's kingdom to come and for him to "deliver us from evil," for our pastors and elders, and to be aware of the antinomian spirit in our own sinful hearts.

> Keep her life and doctrine pure,
> Help her, patient to endure,
> Trusting in Thy promise sure:
> We beseech Thee, hear us.
>
> Be Thou with her all the days,
> May she, safe from error's ways,
> Toil for Thine eternal praise:
> We beseech Thee, hear us.
>
> May she holy triumphs win,
> Overthrow the hosts of sin,
> Gather all the nations in:
> We beseech Thee, hear us.[60]

---

58 Luther, *Sermons*, 203.
59 Calvin, *Jude*, 427.
60 From the hymn, "Jesus, With Thy Church Abide," by Thomas Benson Pollock.

3
Contending by Knowing the Word

Jude 5–10

ର୍ଚ୍ଚ   ୬୬

IN the Oscar-nominated movie, *A Few Good Men* (1992), there is a court scene in which the U.S. government's prosecutor, Captain Jack Ross, is cross-examining a defense witness and asks him to turn in various Marine handbooks to find the term and definition of "Code Red." After the witness says it doesn't exist, Capt. Ross turns around and begins returning to the prosecutor's table when the defense lawyer, Lieutenant Daniel Kaffee, gets up to re-direct, grabs the Standard Operating Procedure Manual out of the hands of Capt. Ross, and asks the witness to find the chapter on the mess hall. The witness says it's not in the manual, but that Marines just know where to go. Lt. Kaffee's knowledge of the Marine manual brilliantly turned the tide of his defense.

We live in a time in which anyone can charge the Christian faith with anything they've made up or can make assertions without having read the Christian's book—the Bible. In Jude's day "certain people" (*tines anthrōpoi*) had "crept in [to the church] unnoticed" and began to pervert the grace of God (v. 4) by saying things such as we hear today, "God made you a sexual being, so enjoy." Jude now turns his attention to these false teachers, their false doctrines, and their false way of living by turning to his knowledge of the Word of God to make his case against them.

If you recall from chapter 1 and the outline of this short epistle, now in verses 5–16 we have the rhetorical section in which Jude marshals his legal defense of his claims—what the Romans called the *probatio*—in order to awaken his listeners to the danger that is already in their assemblies. In verses 5–7 he offers evidence from the written source of the Old Testament and then in verses 8–10 he applies the evidence to these people. Again in verse 11 he offers evidence from the Old Testament and then in verses 12–13 he applies the evidence. One final time in verses 14–15 he offers evidence and then in verse 16 he applies it to the false teachers. We'll take up this material in three chapters.

In particular his evidence comes from the Old Testament. Notice in verse 5 that he says, "Now I want to remind you," which assumes that they already have a knowledge of what he is going to talk about. As God's people we are called to remember individually, recount to our children as families, and also to recount corporately in public worship the mighty works that God has done in the history of the Old Testament, leading us to Jesus Christ. As the Psalmist sung, "Oh give thanks to the LORD; call upon his name; make known his deeds among the peoples! Sing to him, sing praises to him; tell of all his wondrous works! Remember the wondrous works that he has done, his miracles, and the judgments he uttered" (Psalm 105:1, 2, 5). Calvin said, "once we have been called by God, we must not idly glory in His grace, but rather walk circumspectly in His paths."[61] The principle for us is that in order for us to contend for the faith we must know the Word of God. The Jews of Berea received Paul's preaching "with all eagerness, examining the Scriptures [of the Old Testament] daily to see if these things were so" (Acts 17:11). We have not only the Old Testament but also the New Testament as our canon, or, rule of faith and life. In the Word of God we come to know the heart of God opened to us.[62] As Gregory the Great (d. 604) said, "Learn the heart of God in the words of God."[63] In the context of Jude, this means protecting the church from error so that his loving heart would be seen clearly.

So what Jude is going to do, in presenting his evidence that "these people" are ungodly, is really to present evidence, which they already know and then apply it to this particular current situation. At the end of verse 7 he speaks of Sodom and Gomorrah as "an example" (*deigma*) of the punishment of eternal fire. Grammatically these words refer strictly to Sodom and Gomorrah; yet, all three of the examples in verses 5–7 serve as examples of the punishment of the ungodly. As one author said, "The past explains the present and thus foreshadows the future."[64] Here in verses 5–10 Jude equips us to contend for the faith by remembering and applying the Word of God to the task at hand.

Ancient Examples

Jude does this by listing three ancient examples from the Old Testament. As previously, Jude writes in triplets to gain our attention: Israel, the angels, and Sodom and Gomorrah. And if you know your Old Testament even in a cursory way, what should strike you

---

61 Calvin, *Commentary*, 326.

62 Manton, *Jude*, 5:106.

63 *Letter to Theodorus*, 4:31.

64 J. Daryl Charles, *2 Peter, Jude* in *1–2 Peter, Jude*, Believers Church Bible Commentary (Scottsdale, PA: Herald Press, 1999), 291.

about this list of three examples is that Jude marshals them forward as evidence in a non-chronological way. The list should have been: angels, Sodom and Gomorrah, and Israel. Israel should have been last, but Jude places Israel first. Why? He does this in order to arrest the attention of his readers to the situation that existed in their churches just as it did among the ancient people of Israel. This way his hearers and we cannot say, "Well, he's talking about what happened in the spiritual realm of angels and what happened among those pagans in Sodom and Gomorrah." "No," he says, "what I'm going to say to you has happened before and you would recognize this if you knew your Old Testament." That's why he says, "Now I want to remind you, although you once fully knew it" (v. 5).

Israel

Jude reminds his hearers of what they once fully knew about the example of Israel's salvation and then the condemnation of some, their exodus and then the excommunication of some. The ESV says, "*Jesus ... saved a people out of the land of Egypt*" (v. 5). If you have the old King James or New King James or a more modern translation like the NIV or NASB, your Bible reads "Lord." You need to remember that while the original writing of the letter of Jude was inspired by the Holy Spirit (2 Timothy 3:16), the subsequent copying of it was subject to human error. And so the Greek New Testament manuscripts we have do contain what are called "textual variants." These do not negate the fact that we have God's Word today; it just means we have to do hard work to try to determine as best we can, what God said.

The reading "Jesus" is found in the significant manuscripts known as *Codex Vaticanus* (AD350) and *Codex Alexandrinus* (early AD 400s). The "traditional" text behind the King James Version says "Lord." On the other hand, the earliest manuscript we have of Jude is a papyrus scroll P72 that dates from around AD300 and says "God [who is] Christ."

Another option for what has happened is that a scribe miscopied an abbreviation. Ancient scribes would abbreviate what we call *nomina sacra*, sacred names. And so the title "Lord" was abbreviated KS and the name "Jesus" was abbreviated IS. These easily could have been switched in later manuscripts.[65] Scholars debate which of these is the original reading.[66]

Regardless of the precise reading we think is original, I believe it is clear that they are all referring to the same divine Person. If the reading is "Jesus," it's speaking of the Son of God anachronistically. If the reading is "God [who is] Christ," it's speaking of the Old Testament God of Israel being revealed in Jesus who is the Messiah or Christ. And even if the best reading is the more traditional "Lord," notice how this connects to the previous verse 4, in which Jesus is called the Lord and Sovereign. However Jude is saying it, he is clearly saying that the Lord God of Israel in the Old Testament is our Lord Jesus Christ in the New; Israel's Redeemer from Egypt is our Redeemer from sin.

But though all Israel experienced the Exodus, some would afterwards be punished: the Lord "afterward destroyed those who did not believe" (v. 5). The Lord destroyed some by *fire*. We read in Numbers 11 that "the people complained in the hearing of the Lord about their misfortunes, and when the Lord heard it, his anger was kindled, and the fire of the Lord burned among them and consumed some outlying parts

---

65 On *nomina sacra*, see Philip Wesley Comfort, *A Commentary on the Manuscripts and Text of the New Testament* (Grand Rapids, MI: Kregel Academic, 2015), 419–443. In the seventeenth century, Matthew Poole cited Hugo Grotius as one who thought this was a viable explanation. Poole, *Jude*, 231–232.

66 Comfort says "Jesus" or "God [who is] Christ" are most likely the original. *A Commentary on the Manuscripts and Text of the New Testament*, 402, as does Carroll D. Osburn, "The Text of Jude 5." *Biblica* 62:1 (1981): 107–115. Moo follows the traditional reading of "Lord" as referring to the Lord of the Old Testament. *2 Peter and Jude*, 239–240. Schreiner also follows the reading "Lord" but specifies that it refers to the Father. *1, 2 Peter, Jude*, 444–445.

of the camp" (Numbers 11:1). That was not the kind of bonfire party you wanted to participate in! He destroyed some by *plague*. When "the rabble that was among them had a strong craving … and said, 'Oh that we had meat to eat!'" (Numbers 11:4) the Lord sent a plague among them (Numbers 11:31–34). When the spies returned from the Promised Land and gave a faithless report, they too died in a plague (Numbers 14:37). After Korah's rebellion (see below) there was another plague that broke out and killed another 14,700 (Numbers 16:49). The Lord destroyed some by an *earthquake*. In the aforementioned Korah's rebellion, all those who belonged to Korah along with their households were swallowed up by a crack that opened up in the earth (Numbers 16:31–35). The Lord destroyed some by *serpents*. As the people grew impatient again on their journey some "spoke against God and against Moses, 'Why have you brought us up out of Egypt to die in the wilderness? For there is no food and no water, and we loathe this worthless food'" (Numbers 21:4–5). In response the Lord sent "fiery serpents" that "bit the people, so that many people of Israel died" (Numbers 21:6). This ended when they confessed their sin and looked to the bronze serpent on a pole that the Lord commanded Moses to make (Numbers 21:7–9). The Lord destroyed some by the hands of the *Levites*. He did this after Israel created a golden god and worshipped it as the Lord in direct violation of the second commandment (Exodus 32) and he did this after Israelite men entered into sexual immorality with the Moabite woman at Baal of Peor (Numbers 25).

But those destructions were child's play compared with what we read in Numbers 13–14. The Lord would destroy an entire generation of Israelites by *causing them to wander forty years*. After spying out the Promised Land, ten of the twelve spies gave a faithless report that they could not defeat its inhabitants. And when the people rebelled and prepared to stone Moses, Aaron, Joshua, and Caleb, the Lord threatened to kill all Israel. Moses interceded and the Lord forgave, but only temporarily, as those males twenty years and older (except Joshua and Caleb) would die in the wilderness for unbelief. As the Psalm later says, "Therefore I swore in my wrath, 'They shall never enter my rest'" (Psalm 95:11).

This using of Israel as an example of the punishment of the antinomians in Jude's day is also a not-too-subtle warning to us to beware of our own hearts being led astray by the cravings of our sinful hearts. The unbelieving generation of Israel wanted to satisfy their cravings for meat and their homes in Egypt. The ungodly in Jude's day were craving their desires and pleasures. And these ungodly men are held out to us an incentive to live godly lives. Paul makes this comparison and contrast in 1 Corinthians 10:6–13:

> Now these things took place as examples for us, that we might not desire evil as they did. Do not be idolaters as some of them were; as it is written, "The people sat down to eat and drink and rose up to play." We must not indulge in sexual immorality as some of them did, and twenty-three thousand fell in a single day. We must not put Christ to the test, as some of them did and were destroyed by serpents, nor grumble, as some of them did and were destroyed by the Destroyer. Now these things happened to them as an example, but they were written down for our instruction, on whom the end of the ages has come. Therefore let anyone who thinks that he stands take heed lest he fall. No temptation has overtaken you that is not common to man. God is faithful, and he will not let you be tempted beyond your ability, but with the temptation he will also provide the way of escape, that you may be able to endure it.

Angels

Jude reminds his hearers of what they once fully knew about the example of the angels' fall from glory: "And the angels who did not stay within their own position of authority, but left their proper dwelling, he has kept in eternal chains under gloomy darkness until the judgment of the great day" (v. 6). Jude uses a literary pun for ironic effect here when he says that they "who did not stay" (*mē tērēsantas*) in their places of authority are being "kept" (*tetērēken*) in chains until the great day.

The angels that Jude is speaking of refer to what we call fallen angels or demons. They, along with those angels that did not fall, had a position of authority—under the authority of the Sovereign Lord himself. We can call them with Paul, in an ironic way, "powers, rulers, authorities" (e.g., Romans 8:38; Ephesians 6:12; Colossians 2:15). We learn of this fall in some cryptic texts of Scripture, such as Isaiah 14, Isaiah 24, Ezekiel 28, and Revelation 12. The Belgic Confession summarizes this material saying

> He also created the angels good, to be His messengers and to serve His elect; some of whom are fallen from that excellency in which God created them into everlasting perdition, and the others have by the grace of God remained steadfast and continued in their first state. The devils and evil spirits are so depraved that they are enemies of God and every good thing; to the utmost of their power as murderers watching to ruin the Church and every member thereof, and by their wicked stratagems to destroy all; and are, therefore, by their own wickedness adjudged to eternal damnation, daily expecting their horrible torments. (BC, art. 12)

This goodness of the angels' original creation, was in their being created "immortal, holy, excelling in knowledge, mighty in power, to execute his commandments, and to praise his name" (WLC, Q&A 16).

But some of these angels who basked in the light of God's eternal glory and reflected his refulgence now dwell in darkness.[67] They were "permitted" by God "willfully and irrecoverably, to fall into sin and damnation" (WLC, Q&A 19). This is meant to be an example to us, to cause in us a godly fear and trembling. And as we reflect in wonder upon the fall of such awesome creatures, we ought also to be filled with praise, that we who have fallen into sin are rescued from our chains! We, too, have willfully plunged ourselves into their darkness of sin. Yet, our fall was not irrecoverable. As the ancient commentator, Hesychius of Jerusalem (*ca.* fifth c.), said,

> Who can understand God's love for his people or figure out the truth just by his own reasoning? For because of the truth he did not spare the angels who sinned, but on account of his kindness toward us he has allowed harlots and publicans into his kingdom.[68]

Sodom and Gomorrah

Jude reminds his hearers of what they once fully knew about the example of Sodom and Gomorrah: "just as Sodom and Gomorrah and the surrounding cities, which likewise indulged in sexual immorality and pursued unnatural desire, serve as an example by undergoing a punishment of eternal fire" (v. 7). Sodom and Gomorrah (Genesis 18–19) is probably the most common biblical example of human sin and divine punishment. And Jude makes the connection between the angels and these cities of the plain, saying, "Just as" the angels are being kept "in eternal chains under gloomy darkness until the judgment of the great day" (v. 6) so too Sodom and Gomorrah "and the surrounding cities" are an example "by undergoing a punishment of eternal fire" (v. 7).

---

67 Calvin, *Commentary*, 327.
68 *James, 1–2 Peter, 1–3 John, Jude*, ed. Bray, 251.

The text says that they "indulged in sexual immorality and pursued unnatural desire." This latter phrase is literally "other flesh" (*sarkos heteras*). This has been understood from ancient centuries as a way of saying sexual relations other than what is natural, i.e., homosexuality.[69] We see this in Romans 1 where Paul speaks of God's wrath being poured out on societies through the means of homosexuality:

> Therefore God gave them up in the lusts of their hearts to impurity, to the dishonoring of their bodies among themselves, because they exchanged the truth about God for a lie and worshiped and served the creature rather than the Creator, who is blessed forever! Amen. For this reason God gave them up to dishonorable passions. For their women exchanged natural relations for those that are contrary to nature; and the men likewise gave up natural relations with women and were consumed with passion for one another, men committing shameless acts with men and receiving in themselves the due penalty for their error. And since they did not see fit to acknowledge God, God gave them up to a debased mind to do what ought not to be done. (Romans 1:24–28)

Sadly, in the West, we now live in cultures just like ancient Rome, in which sexual immorality, including homosexuality, is tolerated and promoted. The question to ask from Jude is how do the words of verse 7 reveal God's attitude to these "alternative lifestyles?"

Paul says that fallen humanity's idolatry leads to immorality. Unbelievers have exchanged God's glory for the shame of idolatry

---

69 Oecumenius in *James, 1–2 Peter, 1–3 John, Jude*, ed. Bray, 251; Calvin, *Commentary*, 327–328; *Exposition*, 8; Kistemaker, 381–382; Dick Lucas and Christopher Green, *The Message of 2 Peter & Jude: The Promise of His Coming*, The Bible Speaks Today (Leicester, England/Downers Grove, IL: Inter-Varsity Press, 1995), 186–187; Moo, *2 Peter and Jude*, 242, 250–255; Schreiner *1, 2 Peter, Jude*, 451–453.

(Romans 1:23). "Therefore God gave them up in the lusts of their hearts to impurity, to the dishonoring of their bodies among themselves" (Romans 1:24). So-called sexual "freedom" to do what you want to do with your own body is actually bondage to sin. When you think you're as free as God to use the body God gave you for anything you want without any of God's laws, you're actually a slave of sin. And it is this idolatry that leads to immorality, Paul says God actually gives humanity over to it. He abandons humanity to its sins as a judgment in that terrible, threefold refrain: "God gave them up" (Romans 1:24, 26, 28). The ancient preacher John Chrysostom (349–407) said that knowing this we are to shed tears for those given over to homosexuality.[70] These are image-bearers of God whose minds and hearts have been darkened to the knowledge of God. And they have "exchanged the truth about God for a lie" (Romans 1:25) and "exchanged natural relations," meaning, how God created their bodies to be used, for what is "contrary to nature" (Romans 1:26; 27). Homosexuality is turning God's creation upside down.[71] And so we need to love them as we are to love all our neighbors. We are to pray for their conversion.[72]

In response to this we are told that the Bible's teaching on homosexuality is irrelevant because it's pre-modern. It doesn't take into account modern psychology. What's our answer? The Bible is the Word of God, but more to the point, the Bible teaches God's *creational* pattern for human sexuality. We are told that the New

---

70 St. John Chrysostom, *Homilies on Romans*, trans. Panayiotis Papageorgiou (Brookline, MA: Holy Cross Orthodox Press, 2013), 63.

71 Chrysostom, *Homilies on Romans*, 59.

72 I encourage you to read two excellent resources: Sam Allberry, *Is God Anti-Gay? And Other Questions About Homosexuality, the Bible and Same-Sex Attraction* (Epsom: The Good Book Company, 2013) and *The Gospel & Sexual Orientation: A Testimony of the Reformed Presbyterian Church of North America* (Pittsburg: Crown & Covenant Publications and The Synod of the Reformed Presbyterian Church of North America, 2012).

Testament's verses about "homosexuality" are speaking of pederasty, adult males with male children. You'll hear that this was the only homosexuality the Greeks and Romans knew. That's just not true. Even more, the text is about homosexuality and not pederasty because Paul says women have exchanged what is natural, that is, to be with a man, for what is not natural, that is, to be with another woman. We are told that when Paul speaks of "nature" and what it "natural" here these are not universal truths. Why not? What is natural to me may not be for you. How would you respond? The words "natural" and "unnatural" were used in ancient writings to contrast heterosexual and homosexual relations.[73] Even more, here in the text of Romans these words are rooted in the creation as Paul is speaking of things "since the creation of the world" (Romans 1:20) and God as "Creator" (Romans 1:25).

The hope for all sinners in their sins is Jesus Christ. Notice how seriously Paul speaks of sin but also what God does in us to save us in 1 Corinthians 6:9–11:

> Or do you not know that the unrighteous will not inherit the kingdom of God? Do not be deceived: neither the sexually immoral, nor idolaters, nor adulterers, nor men who practice homosexuality, nor thieves, nor the greedy, nor drunkards, nor revilers, nor swindlers will inherit the kingdom of God. And such were some of you. But you were washed, you were sanctified, you were justified in the name of the Lord Jesus Christ and by the Spirit of our God.

And such were some of you. Grace is real. Grace changes us.

Why do we need to know the Word of God so well, including the

---

73 See the discussion in John R. W. Stott, *The Message of Romans*, The Bible Speaks Today (Downers Grove, IL: Inter-Varsity Press, 1994), 77–78.

Old Testament? We need to know our Old Testaments because there is nothing new under the sun. The same errors in the past are around today. And trying to remove these errors from the church without the Word would be like me trying to empty the Pacific Ocean with a shell.[74]

Contemporary Application

Notice here that for Jude, equipping Christians to contend for their faith is not merely giving them true biblical information; it also involves application of that truth to their specific context. Exposition must have application. As Thomas Manton once said of the necessity of current application: "It is but cheap zeal that declaimeth against antiquated errors, and things now out of use and practice."[75] Jude goes on to take these three Old Testament examples and apply them to his hearers' situation when he says, "in like manner" (v. 8; *homoiōs*), or "likewise, similarly."

"These people also" like the unbelieving Israel, the fallen angels, and immoral Sodom and Gomorrah, "relying on their dreams" (v. 8) are doing three things similar to the examples above: they "defile the flesh" like those in Sodom and Gomorrah, "reject authority" like the angels and like Israel, and "blaspheme the glorious ones" like the fallen angels did to the Lord and like the Israelites in the wilderness who did not believe the Lord's leadership team of Moses and Aaron (v. 8).

Why does he say they do this "relying on their dreams?" To call someone a "dreamer" in the Old Testament is to call them a false prophet (Deuteronomy 13:15–5; Isaiah 56:10; Jeremiah 23:16, 32; Zechariah 10:2). In the Old Testament "dreamers" were those who claimed to receive words from God just as true prophets did

---

74 This image is adapted from Manton, *Jude*, 5:107.
75 Manton, *Jude*, 5:103.

via dreams (Deuteronomy 13:2, 4, 6). These infiltrators of Jude's day were claiming to have authoritative, fresh words from God. Sound familiar? How many prophets, apostles, bishops, faith healers, and televangelists today announce a "fresh word" from the Lord—but for a small price? And with their words from their so-called "god" these false teachers went on defiling the flesh. Jude is showing the folly of their lives, saying, in effect, "You're dreaming if you think God has said what you say he has said!"

Just as those in Sodom and Gomorrah defiled their flesh in unclean sexual actions so too these dreamers were doing in the church.[76] This applies to our day when we hear young *Christians* saying things like, "I know I am not married to my girlfriend, but if it was wrong then God would not be blessing us so much." I once knew a group of Christians who had been led astray by one such false teacher. He reasoned his way into thinking that since God ordained everything that comes to pass in this life, and since he desired to come out as a homosexual, therefore God had planned this. And thus whatever sin you want to partake of is allowed by God as well as covered by the blood of Jesus Christ.

These dreamers also reject authority. Just as the angels rejected God's authority, so too these dreamers. Just as the Israelites rejected the Lord's authority, so too these dreamers. People in the church rarely do this directly to God. Instead, they do it by means of rejecting the church's leadership. When concerned members, pastors and elders find out about these sins and confront these professing believers, they will not listen. "I can worship on my own just as well as with the church." "Who are the elders and pastors to tell me how to live? After all, I

---

76 Poole relates the exegesis of a French Roman Catholic theologian, Johannes Gagnaeus (d. 1549), who said the phrase, "defile the flesh," referred to nocturnal emissions. Poole, *Jude,* 237–238.

know them and what's in their hearts." "Religion is simply a way of controlling and manipulating others and I will not be manipulated." Ultimately they reject Christ, the Lord and Sovereign.

Another legitimate application of this text is one the Protestant Reformers such as Calvin and Luther taught. The issue of rejecting authority applies to professing Christians rejecting the God-ordained authority of the civil magistrates.[77] As Paul said, "Let every person be subject to the governing authorities" (Romans 13:1). Why? "For there is no authority except from God, and those that exist have been instituted by God. Therefore whoever resists the authorities resists what God has appointed ... for he is God's servant for your good" (Romans 13:1–2, 4). Because of this, we are to "be in subjection, not only to avoid God's wrath" (Romans 13:5) but also are to "pay taxes" (Romans 13:6).

These people rely on their "dreams" to blaspheme, literally, "glories" (*doxas*), which Clement of Alexandria interpreted as angels.[78] What does this mean? It means that when Israel rejected the Lord, they were doing so by rejecting the angels who delivered the law (Galatians 3:19; Hebrews 2:2). Today this is in the church when people believe they have power to "bind and loose" demons and loose Satanic curses off of their families, and that they can exorcise enemy authority by laying hands on and anointing others as if they were the apostles of the Lord (e.g., Matthew 10:1, 8; Luke 10:9, 17–20).

But Jude shows how foolish this is when he says that even "when the archangel Michael, contending with the devil, was disputing about the body of Moses, he did not presume to pronounce a blasphemous

---

77 Calvin, *Commentary*, 328–329; Luther, *Sermons*, 206.
78 Clement of Alexandria, "Comments on the Epistle of Jude," in *ANF*, 2:573 col. 2. See also Lucas and Green, *The Message of 2 Peter & Jude*, 189; Moo, *2 Peter and Jude*, 244–246.

judgment, but said, "The Lord rebuke you" (v. 9). Not even "angels, though greater in might and power" than us, do this (2 Peter 2:11). The application to draw is how much more so ought we who are sinful beggars refrain from such dangerous spiritual activity. As Calvin said, "Michael simply imposed silence on the devil in the name of the Lord," and so should we.[79] While early commentators wondered where this story came from,[80] we do see allusion to this encounter in the prophet Zechariah (Zechariah 3:2). To engage in such danger is to "blaspheme all that they do not understand" because the unseen realm is just that, unseen (v. 10). And the result is that these false prophets act "like unreasoning animals" and end up in spiritual disaster, being "destroyed by all that they … understand instinctively" (v. 10). In Peter's parallel passage, he called these false prophets "irrational animals, creatures of instinct" (2 Peter 2:12). The point of this striking image is that the false prophets are like animals because they "understand instinctively" (v. 10) the dangers of immorality (v. 7). In other words, like all humans, they know the law of God because it is implanted in their hearts (Romans 1:18–32; 2:12–16). And they know the righteous judgment of God for disobeying God's law. Nevertheless, these false prophets are so "unreasoning" (v. 10) and so "irrational" (2 Peter 2:12) that they live merely as "creatures of instinct" (2 Peter 2:12), following their lusts to their own destruction.

Conclusion: The Key to Our Contention

Let me conclude this chapter by saying that the key to our contention in defending our lives, our families, our churches, and our countries from spiritual danger is knowing the Word of God inside and out. Of the Word of God we sing,

---

79 Calvin, *Exposition*, 9. See also Bede's comments in *James, 1–2 Peter, 1–3 John, Jude*, ed. Bray, 253.

80 *James, 1–2 Peter, 1–3 John, Jude*, ed. Bray, 252–253.

Mine to tell of joys to come,
And the rebel sinner's doom:
O thou holy book divine,
Precious treasure thou art mine.[81]

Calvin said, "Let us heed the simplicity of Scripture with more attention and respect, in case our over-ingenious philosophizing leads us, not to heaven, but rather to the bewildering labyrinths of the depths beneath."[82]

---

81 From the hymn, "Holy Bible, Book Divine," by John Burton.
82 Calvin, *Commentary*, 331.

4
Why is False Doctrine So Bad?

Jude 11–13

ର ෴

ROBERT Louis Stevenson's, *The Strange Case of Dr. Jekyll and Mr. Hyde* (1886), is the story of Dr. Henry Jekyll's attempt to separate himself from his evil impulses. Eventually he discovers a potion that transforms him temporarily into the unconscionable murderer, Mr. Hyde. At first, Jekyll delighted in becoming Hyde because it gave him unbridled, guiltless freedom. But over time, he began to turn into Hyde involuntarily in his sleep apart from the potion, and even once at mid-day, sitting in a park. Then even as Hyde he became more and more desperate to reverse this effect his potion had created. But when he needed more and more potion to reverse the effects, he ran out, could not find the ingredients to make more, and transformed into Hyde—permanently. Dr. Henry Jekyll tampered with what should not be tampered with by creating and taking a potion to free himself from his rational and responsible humanity.

This story relates to the text before us because false doctrine is the spiritually dangerous potion that changes us from what God desires for us into what we desire for ourselves. And if we continue in it, we eventually will find ourselves transformed for good. To use a biblical image, false doctrine sears the conscience (1 Timothy 4:2), locking inside the sense of right and wrong so that a person can do what they like on the outside.

Among the worst things you can be called in today's evangelical Christian setting is a "heresy hunter," guilty of "bibliolatry" because you focus to much on the Word of God, or "all head, no heart," meaning, you talk about theology instead of "just worshipping the Lord." It shouldn't surprise us as people speak of doctrine as "the d-word" that is divisive and overly speculative. The world-known mega-church pastor, Rick Warren, even said back in 2005 that what the church of the twenty-first century needs is a reformation of deeds, not creeds: "You know, 500 years ago, the first Reformation with Luther and then Calvin, was about beliefs. I think a new reformation is going to be about behavior. The first Reformation was about creeds; I think this one will be about deeds. I think the first one was about what the church believes; I think this one will be about what the church does."[83]

Sadly, this attitude that used to be a hallmark of Protestant *liberalism* is now a pious platitude of so-called Bible-believing evangelicals that is fit for a Hallmark card. The classic refutation of this attitude that is still relevant today remains J. Gresham Machen's (1881–1937),

---

83 "Myths of the Modern Megachurch," Pew Forum's Faith Angle Conference on Religion, Politics and Public Life. May 23, 2005. As found at http://www. pewforum.org/2005/05/23/myths-of-the-modern-megachurch/ (Accessed August 3, 2016).

Christianity and Liberalism (1923). Against the idea that doctrine is "dead orthodoxy" while what the church needs is vital and practical living, Machen said,

> After listening to modern tirades against the great creeds of the Church, one receives rather a shock when one turns to the Westminster Confession, for example, ... and discovers that in doing so one has turned from shallow modern phrases to a "dead orthodoxy" that is pulsating with life in every word. In such orthodoxy there is life enough to set the whole world aglow with Christian love.[84]

To pit doctrine against duty, theology against community, faith against life is unbiblical. The apostles certainly did not make such a false dichotomy. For example, Paul spoke of "the truth, which accords with godliness" (Titus 1:1). In other words, the truth of the gospel of Jesus Christ causes us to live a godly life for Christ. This is why our forefathers defined theology saying, "Theology is the doctrine of living unto God through Christ."[85]

This dichotomy is also unhelpful to practical Christian living. I once spoke with a visitor to our congregation, who after a service in which we recited together the Apostles' Creed, said, "I'm looking for a church that lives the Apostles' Creed." My response was simple and tongue in cheek: "How can you live it unless you know it?" How are we to live for God unless we know God? It's the same in relationships.

---

84 J. Gresham Machen, *Christianity and Liberalism* (1923; repr., Grand Rapids, MI: Wm. B. Eerdmans Publishing Company, 1994), 46.

85 This comes from Petrus van Mastricht's (1630–1706), *Theoretico-practica theologia* (1699), I.iii, where he said, *Theologia est doctrina Deo vivendi per Christum.* It is based on a lengthy trajectory of Reformed thought most well-known in Willian Ames', "Theology is the doctrine of living to God" (*theologia est doctrina Deo vivendi*). *Medulla Theologica*, 1.1.

How can a husband and wife live together in love unless they know each other closely and intimately? How can friends have a deep bond of love and trust unless they know each other?

As I said earlier, we must contend for the faith but we must do so without being contentious. It's instructive for us to do this by taking up Jude's letter in such a context as ours. We've seen how biblically he refutes and renounces false teachers and their doctrine. Now we see how firmly he does so, saying, "Woe to them" (v. 11). Like the ancient prophet Jeremiah (Jeremiah 48) and like our chief prophet and Lord, Jesus (Matthew 11:21), Jude pronounces eternal damnation upon false teachers.

How bad is false doctrine? It is bad enough to damn you to hell. In human terms, if an engineer of a building makes a mistake, the building collapses, a lot of money is lost, but more tragically, many people die. How much more serious ought we to be with the spiritual truths of the Word of God? As the ancient commentator, Andreas, said, false doctrine kills souls.[86]

And so as we take up Jude verses 11–13, he equips us to contend for the faith by warning us about the dangers of false teachers and their doctrine.

Examples of False Teachers

In verse 11 Jude again turns to the Old Testament Scriptures to give us three examples of false teachers. To the question of why false doctrine is so bad that he can say, "Woe to them," note Jude's examples.

Cain

First, Jude says the false teachers in the church "walked in the way of Cain" (v. 11). We all know the story of Cain and Abel early in the

---

86 *James, 1–2 Peter, 1–3 John, Jude*, ed. Bray, 253, 254.

Bible in Genesis 4. Abel was a shepherd while Cain was a farmer (Genesis 4:2) Theologically speaking, Cain was a member of the covenant community, a professing member of the visible church, along with his father and mother—Adam and Eve—and his brother, Abel. And as a member of the worshipping community he offered "to the Lord an offering of the fruit of the ground" (Genesis 4:3). Sounds good, doesn't it? A sincere effort to worship God with his heart "in the right place." Then we read what Abel brought: "the firstborn of his flock and of their fat portions" (Genesis 4:4). Then we read the Lord's response to these two offerings: "And the Lord had regard for Abel and his offering, but for Cain and his offering he had no regard" (Genesis 4:4–5). Cain became "very angry" and his "face fell" (Genesis 4:5). In response the Lord told him, "If you do well, will you not be accepted?" (Genesis 4:7)

What was better about Abel's offering? The words used of Abel's offering of a firstborn and of the fat portions are later used in Leviticus of acceptable offerings. When the Israelites heard this in Genesis they would have thought of their sacrifices that God prescribed and that were acceptable. In other words, Cain worshipped the Lord God as he desired, not as God did. It's what Paul would later describe as "self-made religion," or, "will worship" (Colossians 2:23).[87] And why did God require animal sacrifice? Because it involved confession of sin and a substitute being put to death in the place of the sinner. God had already set up this pattern of sacrifice to cover sins in Genesis 3:21, where we read, "And the LORD God made for Adam and for his wife garments of skins and clothed them." Why would Cain not offer what God required? Because he lacked faith. Notice how Hebrews 11:4 describes this: "By faith Abel offered to God a more acceptable

---

87 On this and other texts in relation to worship, see Hyde, *Welcome to a Reformed Church*, 113–129.

sacrifice than Cain, through which he was commended as righteous, God commending him by accepting his gifts. And through his faith, though he died, he still speaks."

And so because Cain's self-determined and faithless offering was not accepted by the Lord, he deceived his brother into thinking he wanted to have a conversation with him out in a field; but then he killed Abel (Genesis 4:8). This is why the apostle John interprets this to mean that Cain was "of the evil one" (1 John 3:12). John goes on to ask, "Why did he murder him? Because his own deeds were evil and his brother's righteous" (1 John 3:12). So what does this have to do with the false doctrine of false teachers? False doctrine is theological murder. It sneaks up upon you in order to kill the soul.[88] Be on guard. Know your Bible. Be intimately acquainted with the sound doctrine expressed in such tried and true documents as the ancient Christian Creeds and the Reformation (Heidelberg and Westminster) Catechisms, (Belgic and Westminster) Confessions, and Canons (of Dort).

Balaam

Jude goes on to give a second example. The false prophets "abandoned themselves for the sake of gain to Balaam's error" (v. 11). In Numbers 22–24 we read of King Balak of Moab who sought to hire the mercenary prophet Balaam to curse Israel, which had massed on his border for war and entry into the Promised Land. Why would he seek to hire Balaam? Because we learn elsewhere that Balaam was a diviner (Joshua 13:22) and as Peter says, he loved gain (2 Peter 2:15). He was a prophet for hire, always going to the highest bidder. Yet the Lord wouldn't listen to him (Deuteronomy 23:4–5) and turned his cursing into blessing (Joshua 24:9ff.). We read later on that he led Israel into idolatry and immorality (Numbers 31:16; Revelation 2:14).

---

88 See Calvin, *Exposition*, 10; Poole, *Jude*, 246.

So why is false doctrine so bad? As we learn from Balaam, it is self-seeking. It is always on the lookout for stray, weak sheep to gather up into a new sheep pen so that the false prophet can gain from them, while leading them into immorality. For example, think of the Roman Catholic Church. Rome's doctrine of sin and penance is a game to grab money out of people's wallets. People go to the Vatican City and Saint Peter's Basilica, taking pictures of what looks to be a timeless building built by philanthropic Italians. No; it was built on the backs of poor Germans who were duped into thinking a single coin could buy their deceased loved one out of purgatory.[89] "But that's in the past now." Back in 1999 Pope John Paul II declared a Jubilee Indulgence to any who made a pilgrimage to Rome.[90] The current Pope, Francis I, has declared an Extraordinary Jubilee Year of Mercy from December 8, 2015, until November 20, 2016. What does one need to do in order to receive forgiveness? Make a brief pilgrimage, for example, to the Holy Door in every Cathedral or in designated churches or travel to Rome and visit the Holy Doors in the four Papal Basilicas. That sounds free, doesn't it? Attached to pilgrimage is the sacrament of reconciliation, or what used to be called "penance," that is, making confession to a priest and doing acts of repentance such as praying the "Our Father" and putting an offering in the offering box. And, just as in the time of the Reformation, if you desire this indulgence for a deceased loved one, you can pay for funeral masses to be said on their behalf.[91]

---

89 See Martin Luther's 27th of his 95 Theses in *The Annotated Luther: Volume 1, The Roots of Reform*, ed. Timothy J. Wengert (Minneapolis: Fortress Press, 2015), 38 cf. Letter from Martin Luther to Albrecht, Archbishop of Mainz, *ibid.*, 47–55.

90 http://www.vatican.va/jubilee_2000/docs/documents/hf_jp-ii_doc_30111998_bolla-jubilee_en.html (Accessed October 14, 2015).

91 "Letter of His Holiness Pope Francis According to which an Indulgence is Granted to the Faithful on the Occasion of the Extraordinary of Mercy." As found at https://w2.vatican.va/content/francesco/en/letters/2015/documents/papa-

Korah

Finally, Jude says the false teachers "perished in Korah's rebellion" (v. 11). We read in Numbers 16 that two hundred and fifty of Israel's leaders perished, after they led a rebellion against the Lord's anointed leadership, Moses and Aaron (vv. 1–3, 31–35).

Why is false doctrine so bad? By leading souls to rebel against their God-ordained pastors, it leads the soul to rebel against God and seek its life in itself. Think of the ongoing struggle in churches where false teachers such as the late Harold Camping (1921–2013) taught that the church age was finished, that all churches were apostate, that Christians should leave their churches and gather around Family Radio instead, and await the Judgment Day on May 21, 2011. Think of the things people say about how the Reformed churches understand the doctrine contained in Romans 9 concerning predestination and election. People cause confusion and misunderstanding in saying "Reformed theology has ... ended up creating a monster of theology that dampens the place of our passion and partnership with God"[92] and even worse, that Reformed theology makes *God* a "moral monster."[93]

The caricatures are many: Reformed theology makes God the author of evil, it makes human beings robots, it is deterministic and fatalistic, and it makes us uninterested in evangelism. They've been around for centuries and they are not going away.

---

francesco_20150901_lettera-indulgenza-giubileo-misericordia.html (Accessed October 14, 2015).

92 Tim Stafford, "The Pentecostal Gold Standard," *Christianity Today* 49:7 (July 2005): 26.

93 Roger E. Olson, *Against Calvinism* (Grand Rapids, MI: Zondervan, 2011), e.g., 23. In response see Michael Horton, *For Calvinism* (Grand Rapids, MI: Zondervan, 2011); "Does Calvinism Make God a 'Moral Monster?'" (16 November 2011). As found at https://www.whitehorseinn.org/blog/entry/general/2011/11/16/does-calvinism-make-god-a-moral-monster (Accessed October 14, 2015).

Metaphors of False Teachers

Jude transitions from biblical examples of false teachers and their doctrine in verse 11 to metaphors for them and their teaching in verses 12–13. Again, these metaphors are meant to warn us about the dangers of false teachers and their doctrine by speaking of what these false teachers are in relation to the church.

First, he calls them "hidden reefs at your love feasts, as they feast with you without fear" (v. 12). The word Jude uses is literally reefs and rocks under the sea that would cause shipwrecks. Spiritually speaking, these false teachers who "crept in unnoticed" (v. 4) were teaching false doctrines that were causing moral shipwreck within the churches.[94] And notice how he describes them doing this. They are "hidden reefs at your love feasts," meaning, at gatherings of believers in which the Lord's Supper was celebrated, they were causing their damage. In other words, false teachers work hard at gaining entrance into the life and fellowship of the church. We as overseers of the church need to be diligent to be on the lookout for such infiltrators.

Second, they are "shepherds feeding themselves." What a striking image. A shepherd is to lead his sheep out to good pastureland so that they can eat (Psalm 23 cf. John 10). Instead, these wolves in sheep's clothing eat. What do they eat? In the words of the ancient prophet Ezekiel, in denouncing Israel's shepherds, "Ah, shepherds of Israel who have been feeding yourselves! Should not shepherds feed the sheep? You eat the fat, you clothe yourselves with the wool, you slaughter the fat ones, but you do not feed the sheep … the shepherds have fed themselves, and have not fed my sheep" (Ezekiel 34:2–3, 8). False shepherds do not feed the sheep; they eat them! That's what false doctrine does. It devours souls.

---

94 On the interpretive issue of whether the word is to be translated as "hidden reefs" or "blemishes" (NIV; KJV "spots"), see Moo, *2 Peter and Jude*, 258–259.

Third, they are "waterless clouds, swept along by winds" (v. 12). Where I live on the coast of San Diego, we do not receive much rain. Often we see cumulus clouds off the coast coming in during the morning. These are the big fluffy white clouds. And when the sunlight hits them, they are a brilliant white. As they grow in the morning we often think we're going to receive some rain, only to be disappointed when they dissolve in the early evening. This is what false teachers and their false doctrine are like. They over-promise the rain, but under-deliver nothing. They have no substance. Their sermons are puffed up with hollow slogans and with zeal without knowledge. As the Proverb says, "Like clouds and wind without rain is a man who boasts of a gift he does not give" (Proverbs 25:14).

And this is an apt metaphor. Like these clouds, false teachers lead astray. Paul contrasts the ministry the ascended Christ has given by his Spirit that is intended "to equip the saints for the work of ministry, for building up the body of Christ, until we all attain to the unity of the faith and of the knowledge of the Son of God, to mature manhood, to the measure of the stature of the fullness of Christ" (Ephesians 4:11–13) with the ministry of false teachers. These teachers keep their listeners in a state of spiritual childhood, and cause them to be "tossed to and fro by the waves and *carried about by every wind of doctrine*, by human cunning, by craftiness in deceitful schemes" (Ephesians 4:14). The verb Jude uses for "swept along" (*paraphero*) is related to the verb Paul uses for "carried about" (*periphero*). False doctrine leads to a faith without substance.

Like these clouds, false teachers cannot mature a believer's faith. The prophet Isaiah described the Lord's word and its purpose with the metaphor of rain:

> For as the rain and the snow come down from heaven and do not return there but water the earth, making it bring forth and

sprout, giving seed to the sower and bread to the eater, so shall my word be that goes out from my mouth; it shall not return to me empty, but it shall accomplish that which I purpose, and shall succeed in the thing for which I sent it. (Isaiah 55:10–11)

Water gives life and maturity to seeds, plants, and trees, causing them to be fruitful. Without water, there is no growth.

We have to be careful as believers that we do not go along with these insubstantial clouds. As pastors and elders, it is our duty to be on the lookout not only for false teachers and their doctrine, but also those susceptible to them. The immature "childish" believer is prone to false doctrine (Ephesians 4:14). The non-content believer whose ears are "itching" always listening for the next best thing is prone to false doctrine (2 Timothy 4:3–4). The gullible believer who is too trusting and therefore easily "carried away with the error of lawless people" is prone to false doctrine (2 Peter 3:17).

The remedy is to "grow in the grace and *knowledge* of our Lord and Savior Jesus Christ" (2 Peter 3:18).

Fourth, they are "fruitless trees in late autumn, twice dead, uprooted" (v. 12). Like a tree that is supposed to bear its fruit in autumn, but has none to yield, and like a barren, leafless tree in "late autumn," false teachers are dead. They have nothing to give. Remember Jesus' teaching in Matthew 7, where he warns of false prophets, saying, "Thus you will recognize them by their fruits" (Matthew 7:20). Now, it is true that false prophets do seem to have fruit at times. Look at all the thousands who flock to their mega-churches and their miracle crusades. The book of Hebrews even describes apostates as those who "have once been enlightened, who have tasted the heavenly gift, and have shared in the Holy Spirit, and have tasted of the goodness of the word of God and the powers of the age to come" (Hebrews 6:4–5).

Yet Jude says it another way. They are absolutely fruitless. And their doctrine leads to fruitless Christian living.

False teachers who peddle false doctrine are "twice dead." Not only are they dead spiritually in this life, but they are "storing up wrath for [themselves] on the day of wrath when God's righteous judgment will be revealed" (Romans 2:5). Clement of Alexandria said these false teachers were "twice dead ... once, namely, when they sinned by transgressing, and a second time when delivered up to punishment, according to the predestined judgments of God."[95] If "it is a fearful thing to fall into the hands of the living God" (Hebrews 10:31), how much more so for false teachers? And if God's ordained ministers are to be "judged with greater strictness" (James 3:1), what does that mean for the false minister?

Fifth, they are "wild waves of the sea, casting up the foam of their own shame" (v. 13). This imagery comes from the Psalms, which describe the enemies of the Lord and his people as waves that crash upon the shore:

God is our refuge and strength,
a very present help in trouble.
Therefore we will not fear though the earth gives way,
though the mountains be moved into the heart of the sea,
though its waters roar and foam,
though the mountains tremble at its swelling. (Psalm 46:1–3)

The floods have lifted up, O Lord,
the floods have lifted up their voice;
the floods lift up their roaring.
Mightier than the thunders of many waters,

---

95 Clement of Alexandria, "Comments on the Epistle of Jude," in *ANF*, 2:573. See also Moo, *2 Peter and Jude*, 260.

mightier than the waves of the sea,
the Lord on high is mighty! (Psalm 93:3–4)

False teachers rage against the God who made them. Look at the false teachers who advocate an "openness of God." Men like Gregory Boyd argue that there are aspects of the future choices of humanity that are unknown to God. Therefore, God can make mistakes because he takes risks.[96] False teachers rage against God's revelation in his Word. Think of how recent professing Bible-believing Christians have gone to extra-ordinary lengths to argue that homosexuality is not a sin.[97] The doctrine of false teachers leads people to rage like waves against God and the clarity of his Word. Paul used this imagery when he exhorted us to grow in the faith "so that we may no longer be children, tossed to and fro by the waves and carried about by every wind of doctrine" (Ephesians 4:14). And the result of this, in Jude's context, was freedom to live a worldly life. But a life freed from the laws of God is exciting today, but will crash and dissipate like a wave tomorrow.

Sixth, they are "wandering stars, for whom the gloom of utter darkness has been reserved forever" (v. 13). The ancients did not have our technology or understanding of the nature of the universe. Jude is describing things in an anthropocentric way, that is, from our vantage point. He's not making a "scientific" claim; he's making an observation from the human perspective. Since we know that stars are not "wandering" across the sky at night, but that the earth is rotating on its axis and revolving around the sun, some commentators think

---

96 Gregory A. Boyd, *God of the Possible* (Grand Rapids, MI: Baker Books, 2001).

97 Matthew Vines, *God and the Gay Christian: The Biblical Case in Support of Same-Sex Relationships* (New York, NY: Convergent Books, 2014). In response, the reader is directed to Robert A. J. Gagnon, *The Bible and Homosexual Practice: Texts and Hermeneutics* (Nashville, TN: Abingdon Press, 2001) and Kevin DeYoung, *What Does the Bible Really Teach About Homosexuality?* (Wheaton, IL: Crossway, 2015).

Jude is describing as a "star" what is really a comet[98] or a shooting star.[99] But I think Jude is describing the "planets."[100] The ancients conceived of the universe as very orderly. There were the fixed stars that moved across the sky in relationship to each other as constellations and there were the "wandering stars" or planets. Jude's point was that just as we look up at night and gaze at the heavenly bodies that look to be moving across the sky, so too these false teachers are not fixed. They are not stable and reliable teachers of God's Word. They are aimless, rootless, and pointless people. And the result of their false doctrine is a rootlessness that ends in destruction. As he said the punishment of Sodom and Gomorrah was like "eternal fire" for these false teachers, now here he speaks of "utter darkness … forever." Again, these are metaphors used to describe different aspects of what eternal punishment will be like. Obviously if there is an eternal fire how can there be eternal darkness? Jude's point is that hell is like these descriptions: constant judgment like a fire and constant separation from the grace and mercy of Almighty God like being in darkness.

Conclusion

Why is false doctrine so bad? The proof is in the pudding. Like the potion Dr. Jekyll took, that seemed so liberating for a time, only to lead to ultimate bondage, so too with false doctrine. And as we look back at the history of the Christian church, we can see the fruits of such false teaching as Pelagianism, with its emphasis on humanity's innocence from birth and totally free will. Especially with the rise of the medieval Papacy, the church became so wedded to the civil affairs of life, that they became one and the same. With the doctrine of the Mass, people were taught to place their trust in the miracle of the

---

98 Martin, "Jude," 70.
99 Green, *The Second Epistle General of Peter and the General Epistle of Jude*, 176.
100 The Greek term is *planētai*. See Moo, *2 Peter and Jude*, 261.

priests, who presented again and again the propitiatory sacrifice of Christ to God. And the list goes on. These errors continue, as do the worldwide effects of Pentecostalism, the Word of Faith Movement, and syncretism between Christianity and indigenous religions. And we wonder why we seem so powerless as a people. We wonder why we feel like we are losing the spiritual battle. We wonder why we cry out in agony, "Maranatha! Come quickly, Lord Jesus!"

In contrast, we long to know the healthful words of Christ:

You are the bread of life, dear Lord, to me,
your holy word the truth that rescues me.
Give me to eat and live with you above;
teach me to love your truth, for you are love.[101]

---

[101] From the hymn, "Break Thou the Bread of Life," by Mary A. Lathbury and Alexander Groves.

5
The Hard Truth of the Second Coming

Jude 14–16

છ   ♋

There's a man goin' 'round takin' names
And he decides who to free and who to blame
Everybody won't be treated all the same
There'll be a golden ladder reachin' down
When the man comes around.
The hairs on your arm will stand up
At the terror in each sip and in each sup
Will you partake of that last offered cup
Or disappear into the potter's ground?
When the man comes around.[102]

---

102 From the song, "When the Man Comes Around," by Johnny Cash.

THE Second Coming of Jesus Christ is the next great event in the ministry of our Lord for which we as the church militant on earth are to be waiting and expecting.[103] Jesus promised he would come again (Matthew 24; Acts 1:6–11). Our lives are to be expectant for his coming, not surprised (1 Thessalonians 5:2–4); we are to live as in the day, not in the night (1 Thessalonians 5:4–5); we are to be spiritually awake, not asleep (1 Thessalonians 5:6); we are to be sober, not drunk (1 Thessalonians 5:7–8). And it's in that mindset that Paul says we are to be "waiting for our blessed hope, the appearing of the glory of our great God and Savior Jesus Christ" (Titus 2:13). The coming of the Lord to earth is also the longing of the church triumphant in heaven:

> When he opened the fifth seal, I saw under the altar the souls of those who had been slain for the word of God and for the witness they had borne. They cried out with a loud voice, "O Sovereign Lord, holy and true, how long before you will judge and avenge our blood on those who dwell on the earth?" Then they were each given a white robe and told to rest a little longer, until the number of their fellow servants and their brothers should be complete, who were to be killed as they themselves had been. (Revelation 6:9–11)

This hope for the Lord to come was expressed in the ancient church's liturgy in the cry, "Maranatha, O Lord, come!" (1 Corinthians 16:22; Didache, ch. 10)

But there is another other side to this coming—one that we do not think much about. It's the side Johnny Cash sung about in the lyrics above, "When the Man Comes Around" (2002). Maybe it's

---

103 On this coming of the Lord being the Second Coming and not the secret "rapture," see Daniel R. Hyde, *From the Pen of Pastor Paul: 1–2 Thessalonians* (Welwyn Garden City, UK: EP Books, 2015), 143–150.

because we are afraid for ourselves, because we're not sure which side of Jesus' coming we'll be on. Maybe it's because it causes us so much pain for others whom we have lost, and for whom we fear the worst. The Second Coming of our Lord Jesus Christ is not only a pleasant truth to the believer; there is a hard truth for the unbeliever. It will be a blessing to some but a bane for others.

When Jesus comes again those "who do not know God" in a saving way and "who do not obey the gospel of our Lord Jesus" will "suffer the punishment of eternal destruction, away from the presence of the Lord and from the glory of his might" (2 Thessalonians 1:9). When he comes again to bring this punishment, for the unbeliever it will not be as a lamb to take away their sins but as a lion to give them the reward of their sins. He will come not as their Savior but as their Sovereign. He will come not to congratulate, "Well done, good and faithful servant" (Matthew 25:21), but to condemn, "You wicked and slothful servant … cast the worthless servant into the outer darkness. In that place there will be weeping and gnashing of teeth" (Matthew 25:26, 30). This is the hard truth of the Second Coming found in Jude 14–16. The Belgic Confession summarizes it in these words: "the consideration of this judgment is justly terrible and dreadful to the wicked and ungodly" (BC, art. 37). On that day, "The hairs on your arm will stand up," as Johnny Cash said.

Jude equips us to contend for the faith, pronouncing to us the hard truth of Jesus' Second Coming not for all unbelievers in general, but in particular for the false teachers he's been writing so passionately against. In verses 14–16 Jude concludes his argument against the false teachers with more evidence and application.

Its Reality
This is a hard truth because of its reality. The Second Coming is as real and certain as Jesus' first coming to earth. Jude begins by calling

the infiltrators "these" again (v. 14). It was about them "that Enoch, the seventh from Adam, prophesied, saying, 'Behold, the Lord comes with ten thousands of his holy ones'" (v. 14).

Let me deal with this citation of Enoch first.[104] If you know your Old Testament well or if you are looking at a study Bible, you should be asking yourself, "Where does Enoch say this in the Old Testament?" It's not in Genesis when he is mentioned in chapter 5. It's nowhere else in the Old Testament in precisely this way. In fact, notice the way Jude expresses this quotation. It is not in the typical New Testament way of citing Old Testament texts, "It is written" (e.g., Matthew 2:5–6) or "the Scripture says" (Romans 10:11).[105]

This means that Jude could possibly be citing what is called an *agraphon*, that is, an unwritten tradition that the Jews passed down over the centuries. An example of this would be in 2 Timothy 3:8 where Paul speaks of Jannes and Jambres who opposed Moses during his ministry in Egypt. Another would be where the writer to the Hebrews describes the differences between the earthly mountain of God's holiness in the Old Covenant and the heavenly mountain to which we go in worship. In the midst of this discussion we read, "Indeed, so terrifying was the sight that Moses said, 'I tremble with fear'" (Hebrews 12:21).[106] A second option is that Jude may have done what other New Testament writers did and compiled several Old Testament texts and allusions and put them into one statement. We read of such statements of the coming of the Lord in Deuteronomy: "The LORD came from Sinai and dawned from Seir upon us; he shone

---

104 See J. Daryl Charles, "Jude's Use of Pseudepigraphical Source-Material as Part of a Literary Strategy." *New Testament Studies* 37:1 (January 1991): 130–145.

105 Moo, *2 Peter and Jude*, 273.

106 F.F. Bruce points to Deuteronomy 9:19 as a possible source. *The Epistle to the Hebrews*, The New International Commentary on the New Testament (Revised edition; Grand Rapids: William B. Eerdmans Publishing Company, 1990), 354.

forth from Mount Paran; he came from the ten thousands of holy ones, with flaming fire at his right hand" (Deuteronomy 33:2). Another example would be when Daniel describes the Ancient of Days upon his throne, saying, "A stream of fire issued and came out from before him; a thousand thousands served him, and ten thousand times ten thousand stood before him; the court sat in judgment, and the books were opened" (Daniel 7:10). The third option is that Jude is actually citing the ancient Jewish book of First Enoch 1:9, which early church fathers such as Jerome (347–420) called "apocryphal"[107]—that is, not Scripture. An analogy would be what Paul does with pagan poetical material. Paul quoted from Epimenides of Crete to say, "Cretans are always liars, evil beasts, lazy gluttons" (Titus 1:12), and to say, "In him we live and move and have our being" (Acts 17:28). He also quoted Aratus, "For we are indeed his offspring" (Acts 17:28). In another place he quotes Menander: "If the dead are not raised, 'Let us eat and drink, for tomorrow we die'" (1 Corinthians 15:32). In other words, the New Testament makes use of unwritten and written sources from throughout the ancient world in the course of their arguments, as the Holy Spirit inspired the process and writings of the apostles. This is not an admission that these sources are inspired, but that in the course of inspired writing, these sources communicated true points the apostles sought to make in a way their hearers would receive. In other words, this is citing texts your opponents receive as authoritative to make *your* point.[108] In the end, as Calvin said, we should not "torment [...] ourselves a lot about the matter."[109] The end result is the same. The Lord Jesus Christ is really coming again on the last day.

---

107 Jerome, *On Illustrious Men*, trans. Thomas P. Halton, Fathers of the Church: Volume 100 (Washington, D.C.: The Catholic University of America Press, 1999), 11.

108 Martin, "Jude," 86.

109 Calvin, *Exposition*, 11.

This reality of the Second Coming of Jesus to judge the living and the dead is found over and over again on the pages of our New Testament. But what Jude is saying here is much more profound than that. The reality of the coming of the Lord to earth to execute final judgment has been expected since after the dawn of human history. After the Fall into sin and just before the Flood, which was God's ancient picture of final judgment on the world, Jude says that Enoch prophesied the ultimate coming of the Lord God himself. Jude says "Enoch ... prophesied" (v. 14), which is consistent with the description of him in Genesis when it says he "walked with God" (Genesis 5:24). This is the language of the Old Testament to speak of him as a true and pious prophet of the Lord. A true prophet had close communion and communication with the Lord. [110]

And notice the tense of Jude's citation, "the Lord *comes*." This is actually a past tense verb. It reflects a certainty that the Lord is coming in the future by saying it has already happened. [111] Perhaps you're reading this book but you're not a believer in Jesus Christ yet. Or if you are, you have many, many family and friends who do not know Jesus Christ as Savior. A true prophet tells the truth even in the face of power that can lead to harm. Jude tells us that. I am telling you that here. Jesus of Nazareth is the most verifiable human being from

---

110 G. Ch. Aalders, *Genesis: Volume I*, trans. William Heynen, Bible Student's Commentary (Grand Rapids: Zondervan, 1981), 140–141; Bruce K. Waltke, *Genesis: A Commentary* (Grand Rapids: Zondervan, 2001), 114–115. This rare phrase is only used in Genesis 5:22, 24, 6:9, and Malachi 2:6. On its use in Malachi, see Douglas Stuart, "Malachi," in *The Minor Prophets: An Exegetical & Expository Commentary*, 3 vols. (Grand Rapids: Baker Books, 2003), 3:1320.

111 This is what is called a "prophetic perfect." Matthew Black, "The Maranatha Invocation and Jude 14, 15 (1 Enoch 1:9)," in *Christ and the Spirit in the New Testament*, ed. Barnabas Lindars and Stephen S. Smalley (Cambridge, U.K.: Cambridge University Press, 1973), 194–196.

the ancient world. He really is. He really came to earth, lived, died, and rose again. Now he's in heaven awaiting his return. He's coming again. It's certain.[112] We don't know when. It could be tomorrow; it could be another two millennia. As one hymn puts it:

Day of judgment, day of wonders!
Hark! the trumpet's awful sound,
Louder than a thousand thunders,
Shakes the vast creation round!
How the summons
Will the sinner's heart confound![113]

He offers himself to you now to forgive your sins so that when he returns he will not see them; he will see himself as his righteousness has been given to us in the place of our sins. Receive him. Do not wait.

Its Reason

The Second Coming of Jesus is a hard truth because of the reason he is returning. Jude tells us at the beginning of verse 15 the reason Jesus is coming again is "to execute judgment on all and to convict all the ungodly of all their deeds of ungodliness that they have committed in such an ungodly way, and of all the harsh things that ungodly sinners have spoken against him."[114]

This is the hard truth that the world around you contradicts every day. The media, schools, and politician all say things like this: "It doesn't matter what you believe, as long as you believe something," or, "All roads lead to heaven," or, "There is no ultimate truth, so whatever is true for you is okay." But never forget that what we believe

---

112 See my sermons "The Case for the Cross" (4/6/2012) and "The Case for the Resurrection" (4/8/2012) at www.sermonaudio.com.

113 From the hymn, "Day of Judgment, Day of Wonders!" by John Newton.

114 On Jesus' coming again to judge, see Hyde, *From the Pen of Pastor Paul*, 215–232.

is determined by God in his Word and not what we want or what the world tells us. And despite all these platitudes, the world in which we live still believes in judgment for bad actions. Scientists talk about every action having an equal and opposite reaction. Popular philosophy says that what goes around comes around. If we believe these are true of our actions in this life, then it's not a stretch to say that there is something more ultimate and eternal about our actions. In the movie, *Gladiator* (2000), the Roman General Maximus motivates his cavalry just before a charge, "What we do in life, echoes in eternity." And if we say this in our culture, how much more so is it true if God says it? And if it is true, it is not just true that we get good things after this life; there is a judgment coming. And Jude has already described this judgment as "the gloom of utter darkness" (v. 13). Now he calls it judgment and conviction.

One helpful summary of what the Word of God teaches about this final judgment and conviction is found in the Belgic Confession:

> all men will personally appear before this great Judge, both men and women and children, that have been from the beginning of the world to the end thereof ... Then the books (that is to say, the consciences) shall be opened, and the dead judged according to what they shall have done in this world, whether it be good or evil. Nay, all men shall give an account of every idle word they have spoken, which the world only counts amusement and jest; and then the secrets and hypocrisy of men shall be disclosed and laid open before all. (BC, art. 37)

As I cited earlier, "the consideration of this judgment is justly terrible and dreadful to the wicked and ungodly."

The reason for the Second Coming is Jesus' final judgment. And note that Jude gives the reason for this. There are just grounds for this ultimate punishment. Jude doesn't just rant like a judgmental street preacher that there are "ungodly" people who will be judged; Jude goes on to substantiate this. Jesus is coming to convict and judge "the ungodly of all their deeds of ungodliness that they have committed in such an ungodly way, and of all the harsh things that ungodly sinners have spoken against him" (v. 15).

The "ungodly" have done "deeds of ungodliness" and have done so "in such an ungodly way." Ungodliness is literally to not worship God. The first commandment in the law of God is, "You shall have no other gods before me" (Exodus 20:3; Deuteronomy 5:7) and the first and great commandment, which our Lord Jesus Christ expressed to summarize God's law is, "You shall love the Lord your God with all your heart and with all your soul and with all your strength and with all your mind" (Luke 10:27). Ungodliness, though, is the opposite of this. But the opposite is not just that a person doesn't worship God and that's it, but that a person worships something in the place of God. Ungodliness is linked to idolatry, which is "to conceive or have something else in which to place our trust instead of, or besides, the one true God who has revealed Himself in His Word" (HC, Q&A 95). Jesus is returning to convict and judge all who refuse to worship the one true God but instead worship and serve themselves.

He's also coming to convict and judge the ungodly for "all the harsh things that ungodly sinners have spoken against him"—him being the Lord Jesus Christ. And this is not just a little slap on the wrist for saying "G_damn it!" here or "Jesus Christ!" there. This is final judgment on those who refuse to acknowledge Jesus as Lord and Savior. This is judgment for refusing to submit to what his Word says is his will for our lives.

As has been his pattern, Jude expresses a general truth and then goes on to apply it in a particular way to the particular false teachers infecting the churches for which he was so concerned: "These are grumblers, malcontents, following their own sinful desires; they are loud-mouthed boasters, showing favoritism to gain advantage" (v. 16). If Christ judges "all" (v. 15) when he returns, how much more so those who claim to speak in Jesus' name? He calls them "grumblers," which was how the Israelites in the wilderness expressed discontent in the Lord (Exodus 16:7–12; Numbers 14:27, 29; 16:41; 17:5, 10). He calls them "malcontents," because instead of following God's "holy and righteous and good" law as his will for their lives, they wanted to "follow [...] their own sinful desires." Jesus calls us to die to ourselves, take up his cross, and follow him wherever he calls us (Matthew 16:24). But false prophets use their position for their own pleasures. Jude calls these false teachers "loud-mouthed boasters." Sound like a false teacher you've heard or seen online? And in their boasts, they "show [...] favoritism to gain advantage" (v. 16).

Our Response

As we meditate on the hard reality and hard reasons for the Second Coming of Jesus, we should have a response. One response is to think: "But I've grumbled against God; I've been a malcontent where God has placed me and have sought my own desires; I've boasted about myself and taken away from God's glory; I've shown favoritism to get ahead." And therefore you reason that you deserve this judgment.

Yes, you and I deserve nothing less than eternal punishment for our sins. Yet your concern is a healthy one. It's a sign of the Holy Spirit's working in your life. If you haven't trusted in Jesus, knowing he is coming again is meant to stir you up and shake you up to the reality of his impending judgment. If you are a believer and are concerned, this is good as well. Perhaps you have fallen a little in your faith lately. Perhaps you're just prone to spiritual struggles due to the grind of day-to-day life.

To all of you I want to say as clearly as possible that the Son of God came from heaven to earth two thousand years ago precisely to live and die in the place of sinners like you and me. The key to spiritual comfort and peace and the resolution of any spiritual anxieties you may have is to be sorry for your sins, to confess them to God, to turn away from them, and to give your life into Jesus Christ's safe keeping. For those who do, the Second Coming is meant to be a further source of assurance that you belong to Christ. I cited from the Belgic Confession earlier on the fearfulness it brings to the unbeliever. Let me cite for you what it also says to us who believe. The consideration of this coming of the Lord is "most desirable and comfortable to the righteous and elect." Why? The Confession goes on to state many reasons:

> Because then their full deliverance shall be perfected, and there they shall receive the fruits of their labor and trouble which they have borne. Their innocence shall be known to all ... the faithful and elect shall be crowned with glory and honor; and the Son of God will confess their names before God His Father and His elect angels; all tears shall be wiped from their eyes; and their cause, which is now condemned by many judges and magistrates as heretical and impious will then be known to be the cause of the Son of God. And for a gracious reward, the Lord will cause them to possess such a glory as never entered into the heart of man to conceive. Therefore we expect that great day with a most ardent desire, to the end that we may fully enjoy the promises of God in Christ Jesus our Lord. (art. 37)

On that day, you who have been delivered from the guilt and penalty of your sins will be delivered from the ongoing corruption and power of your sins. Your "full deliverance shall be perfected."

On that day, you who have served the Lord through many trials and tribulations of family, friends, and the world forsaking you, mocking you, reviling you, and ostracizing you "shall receive the fruits of their labor and trouble which they have borne."

On that day, you who have been called guilty of treason against the State for not worshipping it as supreme, guilty of offending the feelings and lives of those who hate God and Jesus Christ will have your "innocence ... known to all."

On that day, you who have little power in this life, who have barely any possession in this life "shall be crowned with glory and honor."

On that day, you who have been forsaken by family and those you thought were friends in your time of need for advocacy and defense will hear "the Son of God ... confess [your] names before God His Father and His elect angels."

On that day, you who have shed many tears in this life due to the agony of physical pain, sorrow of the loss of loved ones, and general pity on the lost, will have "all tears ... wiped from [your] eyes."

On that day, you whose "cause is now condemned by many judges and magistrates as heretical and impious will then be known to be the cause of the Son of God."

On that day, all your labors for the Lord will receive a "gracious reward" as "the Lord will cause them to possess such a glory as never entered into the heart of man to conceive."

Do you see why we can confess so confidently that "we expect that great day with a most ardent desire, to the end that we may fully enjoy the promises of God in Christ Jesus our Lord?"

"There's a man goin' 'round takin' names," especially the names of false teachers, who will "disappear into the potter's ground," having forsaken the Lord of grace. But we who know his name and are known by him, will be recipients of the fullness of his amazing grace:

> See the Judge our nature wearing,
> Clothed in majesty divine!
> You who long for his appearing
> Then shall say, "This God is mine!"
> Gracious Savior,
> Own me on that day for thine![115]

---

115 From the hymn, "Day of Judgment, Day of Wonders!" by John Newton.

6
Evangelism and the Second Coming

Jude 22–23

୶   ୶

In a July 8, 2010 YouTube video, Las Vegas magician and comedian Penn Jillette discusses the gift of a Bible he received from a fan after one of his shows. If you do not know, Penn is an avowed atheist. As he recounts this experience he says,

> I don't respect people who don't proselytize. I don't respect that at all. If you believe that there's a heaven and a hell, and people could be going to hell or not getting eternal life, and you think that it's not really worth telling them this because it would make it socially awkward—and atheists who think people shouldn't proselytize and who say just leave me alone and keep your religion to yourself—how much do you have to hate somebody to not

proselytize? How much do you have to hate somebody to believe everlasting life is possible and not tell them that?[116]

These are serious words for us to consider from one of the main faces of atheism in our day. Previously we saw in Jude 14–16 the hard truth of the Second Coming of our Lord. The hard truth is that he is coming in judgment for those who are "ungodly" (v. 15). And Jude describes this ungodliness in terms of a lifestyle that is contrary to God's will, "following their own sinful desires" (v. 16), and not confessing the truth of Jesus Christ but instead "harsh things … spoken against him" (v. 15). This judgment is coming upon the entire world. In particular it is coming upon false teachers.

And here is where the Penn Jillette video is illustrative. The fact that this judgment of unbelievers is yet in the future means that God the offended Creator has not given up on the world—and neither should we. We are to respond to this hard truth of what is coming in the future by praying for the lost and evangelizing the lost now. We are to respond to this hard truth of what is coming in the future by opening our mouths and trusting God to supply the words now. We are to respond to this hard truth of what is coming in the future by inviting and bringing the lost to hear God speak in his Word now: "Behold, now is the favorable time; behold, now is the day of salvation" (2 Corinthians 6:2).

In verses 17–23 Jude concludes with an appeal to his readers' emotional response. And here in Jude verses 22–23 we have the theme of evangelism of the wandering and wavering within the church before the Second Coming. In other words, as gospel people we need to share that gospel not only with the lost outside the church but with the struggling inside the church as well. We'll come back to

---

116 https://www.youtube.com/watch?v=6md638smQd8

verses 17–21 in the next chapter because verses 22–23 fit so nicely with what we just looked at in verses 14–16. But there's also a beautiful connection between verse 21 and verses 22–23. Notice that while we are to be "waiting for the *mercy* of our Lord Jesus Christ that leads to eternal life" (v. 21) at his Second Coming, we are now to "have mercy" (v. 22) and "show mercy" (v. 23) on those affected so negatively by false teachers.

While Jude is speaking of contending for the faith against the effect of false prophets on the inside of the church, I do think what he says is applicable to evangelism of those outside the Christian community. This leads us to consider the question of our motivation for evangelism? I was converted in the American Charismatic movement as well as experiencing various kinds of American Pentecostalism and Evangelicalism in the first few of years of my Christian life. I cannot point to a source, but my experience testifies as does many of those I've met over the years who have come out of those movements, that evangelism was done out of fear. I remember hearing a sermon in which the pastor said, "If you're not inviting ten people to church every week, you're not obedient to the Great Commission." But fear is not a sufficient motivation. It leads either to selfishness in the Christian life, as you are going to reap the rewards of all that you are doing spiritually, or it leads to despair, because over time you experience rejection by those ten people a week.

There are better motivations. Ultimately, of course, we would say that we participate in personal evangelism for the glory of God. For example, Jesus said, "Let your light shine before others, so that they may see your good works and give glory to your Father who is in heaven" (Matthew 5:16). And Peter said, "Keep your conduct among the Gentiles honorable, so that when they speak against you as evildoers, they may see your good deeds and glorify God on the day of visitation" (1 Peter 2:12). Here in Jude, we have another biblical motivation: our concern for the salvation of the lost. Do you want that same mercy that you will receive on the day of Christ's Second Coming to be experienced by your family, friends, and neighbors?

As we wait for the revelation of God's final act of mercy to us at the Second Coming, we are not merely to sit around passively waiting for that mercy. Our waiting for ourselves gets us moving for the sake of others. The image of waiting for mercy is passive, but this enlivens us to be active in showing mercy to the lost world. As one hymn states it:

> Call them in! the poor, the wretched,
> Sin-stained wanderers from the fold;
> Peace and pardon freely offer!
> Can you weigh their worth with gold?
> Call them in! the weak, the weary,
> Laden with the doom of sin;
> Bid them come and rest in Jesus!
> He is waiting: call them in![117]

In verses 22–23 Jude equips us to contend for the faith by exhorting us to show mercy on those who are in danger of Jesus' Second Coming. And his exhortation is to do this in various ways depending on the varied circumstances of those in need of mercy.[118]

Mercy on Those in Doubt (v. 22)

The mercy of the Second Coming of our Lord for us equips us to show mercy on several different kinds of people. The first is those who are

---

[117] From the hymn, "Call Them In! the Poor, the Wretched" by Anna Shipton.

[118] Calvin, *Commentary*, 335; *Exposition*, 14. On whether there are two or three categories of people in view, see Moo, *2 Peter and Jude*, 286–289. For an argument that there is one *category* of person but three *clauses* describing them, see Joel S. Allen, "A New Possibility for the Three-Clause Format of Jude 22–3." *New Testament Studies* 44:1 (1998): 133–143.

plagued with doubt: "And have mercy on those who doubt" (v. 22). Keep in mind the immediate context of this saying. Jude is speaking of those who to one degree or another had been persuaded by the false prophets that the faith once delivered is not the true faith. This is so important to understand.

What Jude is doing is following the biblical teaching in which there is not only a distinction between believers and unbelievers, but also distinctions among believers. Some are strong in faith while others are weak. Those who are strong are strong in their commitment to the Lord and his Word. Those who are weak are so in their faith. And one reason why is false doctrine. These weak believers have doubts about whether what they are hearing from their teachers or what they are hearing from false teachers is true. For example, think about someone you know who has been taught the truths of the Word of God, but then along comes Mormon missionaries at their door or the local representatives of the Jehovah's Witnesses. They knock on the door, they catch people off guard, and they prey upon the weak believer. Or think about professing believers who turn on the television on a Sunday when they are at home sick, only to hear a very happy, upbeat, positive message from what we know as a "prosperity preacher." Then the doubts begin to set again about basic biblical doctrine, preaching, and worship.

Sadly, every pastor I know including myself, and I would venture to guess every believer out there, has some experience with this. My congregation started with several families in a living room. One of the young men was a former missionary. He read a lot of theology books. He looked as solid as they came. Then he took one introduction to philosophy class at a local junior college and his faith was spinning. "How can we know anything?" was the outcome. I still remember the last time I spoke with him. His final words were, "I wish I had your certainty." Sadly, he plunged into debauchery and eventually committed suicide, leaving a wife and two beautiful children behind. He died in doubt.

What should our response be to the doubter? Jude says, "have mercy" (v. 22). In a very simplistic way, mercy is not getting what you deserve. We deserve eternal death, but God does not give us that but instead he gives eternal life. That's mercy. As pastors and as concerned members, when a professing believer has doubts our response is not to be like a spiritual bounty hunter, tracking down the lost like a convict to be forcibly seized. God does not call us to be heresy hunters. Instead, he calls us to be patient, compassionate, and concerned for the doubter. As Paul said to Timothy, "the Lord's servant must not be quarrelsome but kind to everyone, able to teach, patiently enduring evil, correcting his opponents with gentleness" (2 Timothy 2:24–25a). Why? "God may perhaps grant them repentance leading to a knowledge of the truth, and they may come to their senses and escape from the snare of the devil, after being captured by him to do his will" (2 Timothy 2:25b–26).

This truth applies to our relationships outside of doubters within the community of believers to those who have yet to commit their lives to Jesus Christ because of doubts. There are so many people out there that have never heard the truth of the Word of God clearly presented. There are so many people who have been confused and confounded by every kind of religion, philosophy, and popular idea under the sun. And many of them have serious doubts and serious questions about biblical Christianity. I recall a young woman who was a co-worker of a member in my congregation. She was invited to an Easter service. She left angry. Her anger was not at the message. Her anger was that people actually believed the message! That led her to question and wonder why. She came back many, many months later.

We met, we exchanged emails with questions and answers, and then she started attending, cautiously, but with a genuine interest. I, and others, showed her mercy in the form of listening to her concerns and responding to them with the truth of the Word shared with love. She eventually made a profession of faith.

Mercy on Those in the Fire (v. 23a)

The second kind of people Jude equips us to show mercy upon in light of the Second Coming of our Lord are those who seem to us already close to the fire of hell: "save others by snatching them out of the fire" (v. 23). "Fire" is an image used throughout the Scripture of the judgment of God. For example, in the Old Testament fire is the judgment upon Sodom and Gomorrah (Genesis 18–19), signifying the wrath of God himself. As well, in the New Testament, Paul speaks of the final judgment and the Second Coming of Jesus with this image. When "the Lord Jesus is revealed from heaven with his mighty angels [it will be] in flaming fire, inflicting vengeance on those who do not know God and on those who do not obey the gospel of our Lord Jesus" (2 Thessalonians 1:7–8).

The fire of God's final judgment is now on the horizon. It is like looking to the east, early in the morning just before the first rays of the sun burst over the horizon. What do you see at that moment? You see a faint glow. You know the light is there; it's just a matter of time. So it is with the return of our Lord. This imagery of saving sinners by "snatching them out of the fire" (v. 23) comes from the Old Testament Jude knew so well. We read in the prophecy of Amos that Israel had been saved out of the fires of the Lord's judgment:

> I overthrew some of you,
>   as when God overthrew Sodom and Gomorrah,
>   and you were as a brand plucked out of the burning;
>   yet you did not return to me, declares the Lord. (Amos 4:11)

What is Jude saying to us? There were some in his time that were so close to the flames of hell itself because they were dabbling in the false prophets' teaching of libertinism. Their false doctrine had practical ramifications. Because of what Jude says, how are we as genuine, concerned believers to respond? Jude urges us in no uncertain terms to snatch these kinds of believers out of the impending fires of the coming judgment. Listen to what John Calvin said of these people who were so close to the fire:

> … where there is danger of burning, we do not hesitate to take violent hold on a man we want to bring out unhurt; it would not be enough to beckon with a finger, or politely hold out one's hand, for we must care for their salvation with the thought that, unless they are roughly handled, they will not come to God.[119]

My earliest Christian mentor was a fireman and one of my elders currently is a fireman and some of the stories they've told me are apropos to Jude's image here. As you may well know, there are times in a fire in which a fireman must enter the burning building. Here in San Diego, there are times in which huge sections of our county are burning, and fireman must get in the middle of the conflagration. I've been told that there are times in which people in the midst of the fire's raging inferno will not leave. Some are petrified with fear, others are just downright foolish. For example, when a raging fire is engulfing hills, trees, brush, and entire neighborhoods, some people think jumping in their pool is going to save them. And when the fire department arrives they have to jump in and forcibly remove people or else they will either boil to death or suffocate because the fires consume all the oxygen in the atmosphere. Jude is telling us that there are times in which we must enter into the realm of the fires engulfing

---

119 Calvin, *Commentary*, 335.

these professing Christians. We must engage them. We must even at times physically remove them from a situation in order to save them from eternal doom.

As with before, if this is true of professing believers within the community, how much more so is this true of unbelievers? "But it's so dangerous. How can I ever be the one to get into his or her life and be used of God to save them?" I know that fear; we all do. But we often say things like this because of the fear. We end up sounding like Moses, who, right after the Lord appeared in a burning bush and promised to save Israel from Egypt through Moses, he made up excuses: "But behold, they will not believe me or listen to my voice, for they will say, 'The Lord did not appear to you'" (Exodus 4:1); "Oh, my Lord, I am not eloquent, either in the past or since you have spoken to your servant, but I am slow of speech and of tongue" (Exodus 4:10); "Oh, my Lord, please send someone else" (Exodus 4:13).

People go to hell. People you knew have gone to hell. People you know are on their way. That's reality. Does that reality do anything to your heart? If yes, then you need to enter the fire of their lives. How can you do this? Start by praying. Pray for God to prepare the ground of their hearts with his Holy Spirit to hear the gospel (Matthew 13:1–9, 18–23). Pray for God to crack open a window in their life so you can get in. Maybe the opening is your kids and school. Maybe the opening is sports and participating in them. Maybe the opening is going into your front yard on Saturdays and doing yard work. There are so many potential little openings; pray the Lord opens one up and you see it clearly. Pray for God to give you courage to speak the truth when the time comes. And when the time comes, ask questions, have a conversation, listen, and speak as you are led. Open your mouth and tell them about the things you are learning from the Word of God. Tell them the simple Gospel. Tell them there is more to be heard at your church. Invite and offer to bring them to your church. Give them a Bible. Read the Bible with them. And at the end of the day, pray some more that the Lord would grant them faith so that they grab hold of Christ for rescue with heartfelt faith and love.

Let me also exhort you. Personal evangelism is an area in which we modern-day Christians need to repent and then go forth doing the works God commands us to do. We need to repent of our spiritual laziness, our unconcerned attitudes, and our unwillingness to engage the lost. Like me, you may have come out of a church in which evangelism was used to make you feel guilty so that you would join an evangelistic activity. And you may now look back and think that church did evangelism in every possible wrong way. But let me say that to their credit, they were zealous to see the lost saved. To their credit they were actually doing something about it. Even if their zeal was without knowledge, this does not negate the need for zeal. We need knowledge *and* zeal. What are we doing to evangelize? We need to tell God we're sorry for not caring about souls as he does and then we need to go forth into the world and seize every opportunity to engage family, friends, and neighbors with the terror of the law and the comfort of the gospel.

Mercy on Those in Sin (v. 23b)
The third kind of people Jude equips us to show mercy upon in light of the Second Coming of our Lord are those who are living in sin: "to others show mercy with fear, hating even the garment stained by the flesh" (v. 23). Remember that verse 4 said these false prophets "pervert[ed] the grace of our God into sensuality." They turned the liberty of the gospel into a license for ungodliness, immorality, and selfishness. And what Jude is saying is that there are some people in the visible church that we are going to come into contact with that are in the midst of living this very way. And Jude illustrates this by

saying their garments are "stained by the flesh." They have partaken of this false doctrine and philosophy and it has led them to defile themselves practically.

What this illustrates for us is the mess that the church of Jesus Christ is in. We confess in the Apostles' Creed that the church is "holy." We confess this because of such glorious texts as Ephesians 5, where Paul says Jesus Christ died for the church "that he might sanctify her, having cleansed her by the washing of water with the word" (Ephesians 5:26). And in the very next verse he says Jesus did this "so that he might present the church to himself in splendor, without spot or wrinkle or any such thing" (Ephesians 5:27). The church is holy already in this life and in the life to come it will experience a fullness of that holiness. But in this life, it is also full of sin. We have to understand that our confession of the holiness of the church does not mean it is not still tainted by sin in its day-to-day struggles. There's a distinction between what we are in principle in Christ and what we are practically. This is one of the hardest realities to live with as believers. It is one of the hardest things new elders have to face in a church like mine. A man becomes a member, then matures over some time, and eventually may be ordained to serve as an elder. As the saying goes, "Ignorance is bliss." Once becoming an elder he comes face-to-face with the sin in the church. He has to talk with men and women he thought he knew, but only now does he really know them, as they struggle with pornography, gambling, marital fighting, neglect of children, and the list goes on. The church is a mess; but it's God's mess.

And oftentimes this mess is created by false teachers giving professing believers a false sense of eternal security. So they rest secure in their sins. How should we respond in a godly way? On these believers living in sin we are again to "show mercy" but his time Jude adds with "fear." We are to be merciful, but we are also to be fearful.

What does he mean? He is saying that as we minister to those in sin, we need to be aware that we do not become defiled by them or their lifestyle. How easy it is to minister to a couple that is fighting within their marriage but then you come along to offer godly counsel, only to be tempted yourself to flirt, to entrust your marital secrets, and even to engage in illicit activity. Like Jesus befriended tax collectors, drunkards, and prostitutes, we are to fearfully bear witness to those living in sin, even going into the place of their sin to draw them out. But we're not Jesus. We're sinners. So beware that you do not get caught up in the sins of those you are sharing the good news with.

The simplest way I can state it is to adapt an adage I learned in Charismatic churches: love the sinner but hate the sin. That is what Jude is saying at the end of verse 23: "hating even the garment stained by the flesh." We are to hate the garment the one we are ministering to is wearing and even our own garment as it may get stained. How do we do this? With a person who professes Christ yet is mired in sin, John Calvin said we are to use the law of God with them. We are to show mercy, but with fear. This kind of person needs to hear God's voice in the law, which forbids and commands. And by the terror that the law threatens, to snatch him or her out of sinful lifestyle they are in.[120]

Conclusion

What honesty Jude gives us here: Jesus is coming again. What practicality Jude gives us here in our dealings with fellow Christians and even with the world. Jude is saying to us that when Jesus Christ comes again, every single unbeliever that we know will be swept up in a flood of flames. The question for us is what are we going to do in response?

---

120 Calvin, *Commentary*, 335; *Exposition*, 14.

This reality is one of the hardest things to believe and come to grips with as a Christian. The reality is that many of our loved ones and friends will spend eternity apart from us, apart from the Lord's grace but in the presence of his wrath because of their ungodliness. But the Lord is merciful. So show mercy. Be a people of mercy.

Again, as Penn Jillette said, "how much do you have to hate somebody to *not* proselytize? How much do you have to hate somebody to believe everlasting life is possible and not tell them that?" John Owen (1616–1683) described those whose minds were so affected by sin that they did not believe as being tossed around in a stormy sea. He then asked, "is it humanity to stand on the shore, and seeing men in a storm at sea, wherein they are every moment ready to be cast away and perish, to storm at them ourselves, or to shoot them to death, or to cast fire into their vessel, because they are in danger of being drowned?"[121]

---

121 John Owen, "*Sunesis Pneumatike* or The Causes, Ways, and Means of Understanding the Mind of God as Revealed in His Word, with Assurance Therein," in *The Works of John Owen*, ed. William H. Goold, 16 vols. (1850–53; repr., Edinburgh: The Banner of Truth Trust, fifth printing 1995) 4:177.

7
Four Keys to Contending

Jude 17–21

❧   ❧

TIME and time again, history tells us of Roman legions being far outnumbered by their enemies, only to come away with victory. Among the many reasons for this was the Romans' discipline and training. In the ancient Greek historian Polybius' (200–118BC) work, *The Histories*, we learn about the legions' legendary—and brutal—discipline. In the case of a desertion during battle among a maniple (base unit of 120) we read, "the officers refrain from inflicting the bastinado or the death penalty on all, but find a solution of the difficulty which is both salutary and terror-striking."[122] The "bastinado" (Latin, *fustuarium*) was a capital punishment administered by all the soldiers of the legion hitting a man with sticks and stones. Since the officers could not wipe

---

122 Polybius, *The Histories*, 38.1. As found at http://penelope.uchicago.edu/Thayer/E/Roman/Texts/Polybius/6*.html.

out the entire maniple, "The tribune assembles the legion, and brings up those guilty of leaving the ranks, reproaches them sharply, and finally chooses by lots sometimes five, sometimes eight, sometimes twenty of the offenders, so adjusting the number thus chosen that they form as near as possible the tenth part of those guilty of cowardice."[123] Then came the bastinado while those allowed to live were given rations of barley instead of wheat and had to encamp outside the legion's camp.

As members of Christ's army of faith, such brutal corporal discipline and training doesn't apply directly to us. However, it's this kind of commitment that applies to us in terms of how we live our lives in the face of the world of mocking, scoffing, and unbelief. It's may be easy for us to think of our life of witness and evangelism as charging headlong into fighting for the faith and evangelizing one hundred percent of the time everywhere we are. But this would be foolish to communicate as pastors and as people to receive. Like the ancient Roman legions, we need to prepare and train for the spiritual contention before us. And after such preparation, then we are ready to fight. And as we go out to fight, we rely on our training, which taught us that we may even need to intentionally retreat from time to time behind the walls of the church to rest and recover. If we are not disciplined enough to do that, we may become casualties.

In Jude 17–21 we read about four keys to contending in which we are to train.[124] Jude uses two main verbs here. The first is "remember" the Word (v. 17), which we have already seen and to which we will come back in a moment. The second is "keep yourselves in the love

---

123 Polybius, *The Histories*, 38.2.

124 Andrew J. Bandstra has a helpful little article on how verses 17–23 connect back to verse 3 as the main purpose of this letter. "Onward Christian Soldiers—Praying in Love, with Mercy: Preaching on the Epistle of Jude." *Calvin Theological Journal* 32 (1997): 136–139.

of God" (v. 21). This verb has three others subordinate to it, which explain how we are to keep ourselves in the love of God[125]—both his love for us and our love for him.

Verse 21 really is an amazing thought to pause on for a moment. At the very beginning of this letter Jude described us as "beloved in God the Father" (v. 1). This is our secure status. Why? Because the God who is unchanging (Malachi 3:6) loves us with an unchanging, everlasting love: "I have loved you with an everlasting love" (Jeremiah 31:3). And even in times of lament, we can pray with Jeremiah: "The steadfast love of the LORD never ceases; his mercies never come to an end" (Lamentations 3:22). We can pray with David, "Your steadfast love, O LORD, extends to the heavens, your faithfulness to the clouds … How precious is your steadfast love, O God!" (Psalm 36:5, 7) So secure and stable, firm and fixed is God's love towards his children, that the oft-depressed poet, William Cowper poetically described this love when he said,

> Mine is an unchanging love,
> Higher than the heights above,
> Deeper than the depths beneath,
> Free and faithful, strong as death.[126]

So we know that this is the love we have experienced, are experiencing, and will forever experience from our heavenly Father. But now Jude says to the beloved, "*keep yourselves* in the love of God." We have a position in God's love; now we are to practice that love. We are to persevere in that love. As John tells us, "We love because he first loved us" (1 John 4:19). This is such an illuminating text for our life in Christ, both being preserved by God's love and needing to

---

125 Schreiner, 481.
126 From the hymn, "Hark, My Soul, it is the Lord!" by William Cowper.

persevere in that love. And it is that love of God for us that activates our love for him. There is no "let go and let God" in the Christian life, to use the once popular Christian bumper sticker slogan. As Ralph Martin commented,

> The twin sides of Christian truth are here displayed, in line with Jude's strong theocentric belief that God is in charge of his people's destiny in all ages and has a final purpose in view, which is to "keep [them] from stumbling and to make them stand without blemish in the presence of his glory with rejoicing" (24). Yet these same people are not to be negligent and wayward like unbelieving Israel (5) or unstable and gullible adherents (22–3). The danger that threatens in the alien teaching should awaken them to their peril and alert them to their responsibility, which is to stay within the orbit of divine love and not stray into ruin, as warning examples illustrate (11).[127]

And so, secure, as the army of the Lord, we are called to an ongoing agonizing for the souls of sinners as we fight against the forces of unbelief. And Jude equips us with the keys to victory.

Remembering

The first key to our contention is in verse 17: "But you must *remember*, beloved, the predictions of the apostles of our Lord Jesus Christ." The idea of "remember" in biblical terminology is not merely an intellectual exercise. It involves the will. It leads to action. For example, in Deuteronomy 4 Moses addresses a new generation of Israelites as if they had been at Mount Sinai a generation before, calling them to remember what happened there. And because of what they "recalled" they were actively engaged: "Only take care, and keep your soul diligently, lest you forget the things that your eyes have seen, and

---

127 Martin, "Jude," 79.

lest they depart from your heart all the days of your life. Make them known to your children and your children's children (Deuteronomy 4:9–10).[128]

What are we to "remember" so that we can act? We saw earlier that we are to know the Old Testament well; now Jude specifies "the predictions of the *apostles* of our Lord Jesus Christ." Notice that Jude is speaking about the "the apostles" as a group distinct from himself. And what he says about them making "predictions" was now happening in his hearers' time. Therefore we too need to remember the words of Scripture and be stirred to action. And finally, note the close connection between the apostles and Jesus. They are "apostles *of* our Lord Jesus Christ." Their authority and reliability to predict anything is derivative of their relationship to the Lord. Recall the qualifications of what constituted an apostolic replacement for the traitor Judas. It was to be a man "who … accompanied [the other apostles] during all the time that the Lord Jesus went in and out among us, beginning from the baptism of John until the day when he was taken up from us" (Acts 1:21–22). And we see that all throughout the Gospels from Jesus choosing these particular disciples, to his walking up and down Judea with them, to his teaching them privately as well as their hearing him teach the crowds publicly.

What did they predict? "They said to you, 'In the last time there will be scoffers, following their own ungodly passions'" (v. 18). Here, as I mentioned earlier concerning New Testament writers gathering up several texts and making a statement out of them, Jude summarizes many sayings and texts into one. There are several to take notice of.

---

128 On how Deuteronomy 4 and other Old Testament texts recount the history of salvation to various audiences and generations, see Paul R. House, "Examining the Narrative of Old Testament Narrative: An Exploration in Biblical Theology." *Westminster Theological Journal* 67:2 (Fall 2005): 229–245.

Paul gave a farewell address to the Ephesians elders saying in part, "I know that after my departure fierce wolves will come in among you, not sparing the flock; and from among your own selves will arise men speaking twisted things, to draw away the disciples after them" (Acts 20:29–30). The image of wolves attacking sheep, or false teachers infiltrating the church, comes from our Lord's teaching in John 10. Why do these "wolves" infiltrate the church both from outside as well as inside? They desire "to draw away the disciples after them." Notice that. False teachers use false doctrine to draw people to themselves and not to Christ. This is the "ungodly passion" of which Jude spoke.

Paul would later write back to the pastor of the Ephesian church, Timothy, saying this:

> Now the Spirit expressly says that in later times some will depart from the faith by devoting themselves to deceitful spirits and teachings of demons, through the insincerity of liars whose consciences are seared, who forbid marriage and require abstinence from foods that God created to be received with thanksgiving by those who believe and know the truth. (1 Timothy 4:1–3)

Jude spoke of "the last time" that Paul spoke of. And in that time—which is the time until the Second Coming and not some special period at the end of human history—there would be "deceitful spirits and teachings of demons" manifest "through [means of] the insincerity of liars," whose "ungodly passion" was to get people to follow them in false piety.

Again Paul wrote to his former missionary companion, Timothy, at the end of his life in a Roman prison, speaking of "the last days" in terms of false teachers and their teachings, saying,

> ...there will come times of difficulty. For people will be lovers of self, lovers of money, proud, arrogant, abusive, disobedient to their

parents, ungrateful, unholy, heartless, unappeasable, slanderous, without self-control, brutal, not loving good, treacherous, reckless, swollen with conceit, lovers of pleasure rather than lovers of God, having the appearance of godliness, but denying its power. Avoid such people. (2 Timothy 3:1–5)

Jude merely summarizes the false teachers' motives as "following their own ungodly passions," but Paul spells it out. At first read it might sound like Paul is speaking in general of all humanity outside of Jesus Christ as in Romans 1:28–32. And this is true. But then he gets more specific and applies this to certain men:

> For among them [the "people" of verse 1] are those who creep into households and capture weak women, burdened with sins and led astray by various passions, always learning and never able to arrive at a knowledge of the truth. Just as Jannes and Jambres opposed Moses, so these men also oppose the truth, men corrupted in mind and disqualified regarding the faith. But they will not get very far, for their folly will be plain to all, as was that of those two men. (2 Timothy 3:6–9)

You can hear in the above words where Jude got his imagery, under the inspiration of the Holy Spirit. The false teachers Jude spoke about who "crept in unnoticed" (v. 4; *pareisdunō*) are those Paul speaks of here who "creep into households" (*endunontes eis tas oikias*). And these whom Jude said followed their own ungodly "passions" (*epithumias*) are those whom Paul said were swayed by all kinds of "passions" (*epithumias*).

So Jude is alluding to the apostle Paul's predictions. He's also alluding to the apostle Peter's predictions. Because Jude resembles 2 Peter so much, in the history of exegesis some have had the attitude of Martin Luther: "Nor does it contain anything special beyond pointing to the Second Epistle of Saint Peter, from which it has borrowed nearly all the words."[129] We hear Jude's distinct voice throughout, even when he is relating some of Peter's own words.

> This is now the second letter that I am writing to you, beloved. In both of them I am stirring up your sincere mind by way of reminder, that you should remember the predictions of the holy prophets and the commandment of the Lord and Savior through your apostles, knowing this first of all, that scoffers will come in the last days with scoffing, following their own sinful desires. They will say, "Where is the promise of his coming? For ever since the fathers fell asleep, all things are continuing as they were from the beginning of creation." (2 Peter 3:1–4)

What's interesting about Peter's prediction is how he relates the remembering of the apostles' and the Lord's words in the last days in which there are scoffers particularly to the Second Coming of Jesus. Based on Jude's teaching we see that this scoffing was a denial of the coming of Jesus as Judge because the false teachers had what we call an over-realized eschatology.[130] This means that they thought the things still ahead in the future had already come to pass. And so because believers had everything they would ever have, there was nothing more ahead for them. This led to thinking that ungodliness did not nullify grace and thus liberty became a license. But it's that coming of the Lord that Jude is so bold to proclaim against ungodliness that causes us to be so concerned for the sake of the lost.

Why are we to know the words not only of the Old Testament (vv. 5–16) but also of the New Testament (vv. 17–18) so well? If we don't, we cannot contend. Notice how contentious our opposition

---

129 Luther, *Sermons*, 203.
130 Martin, "Jude," 72–75.

is: "It is these who cause divisions, worldly people, devoid of the Spirit" (v. 19). False teachers divide your church. Are you going to let them? False teachers are worldly. Are you going to let them lead your church from the ways of the Lord to the ways of the world? Being "worldly people" (*psuchikoi*) is the opposite of being Spirit-filled and Spirit-led people. As those "devoid of the Spirit" false teachers are not regenerated; they are natural or unspiritual men and women (1 Corinthians 2:14–16). Are you going to let them take over so that eventually Jesus Christ removes the lampstand of his Holy Spirit from your church (Revelation 2:5)? Know the Word so that you can contend in a Spirit-filled manner without being contentious like the Spirit-less false teachers of the age.

Building

The second key to our contention is "building yourselves up in your most holy faith" (v. 20). This is the first subordinate verb that explains how to "keep yourselves in the love of God" (v. 21). We are to keep ourselves in the love of God by building ourselves up in our faith. Here Paul uses imagery of construction.

Just as with the truth that you are "beloved in God" (v. 1) and are to "keep yourselves in the love of God" (v. 21), so too with the idea of building. The New Testament tells us in many places that it is a reality of our Christian experience that we are already built. Paul says we are "rooted and built up in [Christ] and established in the faith, just as you were taught, abounding in thanksgiving" (Colossians 2:7). Peter also tells us that it is God who is doing the building: "you yourselves like living stones are being built up as a spiritual house, to be a holy priesthood, to offer spiritual sacrifices acceptable to God through Jesus Christ" (1 Peter 2:5). Here, though, Jude is telling us of the practical side that we are to be engaged in. We can think of it like this. When Jesus Christ saved us, he established us upon himself as a foundation.

And now by his Holy Spirit he is building up the structure, the walls, and the roof of our life in Christ. And Jude is saying that the means by which the Spirit does his building work is through us. Again this points to the wonderful truth that our once-for-all salvation in Jesus Christ is what activates our hearts, souls, minds, and strength to work out our salvation with fear and trembling precisely because it is God who is working within us (Philippians 2:12–13). So while the church is described as a temple (1 Corinthians 3:9) it is also being built into a temple (Ephesians 2:20–22). And we participate in that building project. Believers "should not rest satisfied in what measure of faith they had already attained, but still be improving it, and making further progress in it, not only hold fast the truth of the gospel, the right foundation on which they had begun to be built, but get themselves, by the due study and meditation of the word, more and more confirmed in the belief of it."[131]

As we build up ourselves in the faith, we come to know God's love for us; as we come to know God's love our love for him grows. And we need to know his love in the spiritual fight we find ourselves in. We are going to be constantly assaulted with the slanders that either God does not or cannot love us because of our sins or that we really do not love him as evidenced by our inconsistent lifestyle. How do we build ourselves up? I think the key is in the previous verses. We build ourselves up by means of the Word of God: "remember … the predictions of the apostles of our Lord Jesus Christ" (v. 17). Elsewhere, Paul says it like this: "And now I commend you to God and to the word of his grace, which is able to build you up and to give you the inheritance among all those who are sanctified" (Acts 20:32). The Word of God's amazing grace in the gospel is what makes it possible to build ourselves up. Elsewhere the Word is described as the seed that gives

---

131 Poole, *Jude*, 265.

life to our soul (1 Peter 1:22–25) and as the milk that nourishes our soul (1 Peter 2:1–3), but here Jude describes the Word, as the mortar that is used to build up the edifice of our soul upon the foundation of Jesus Christ. Oecumenius said we are to be "forever reforming [ourselves] according to the Holy Spirit's guidance; in other words, by building congregations up, by their preaching, in the teaching of the Holy Spirit."[132]

Praying

The third key to our contention is to "keep yourselves in the love of God" (v. 21) by "praying in the Holy Spirit" (v. 20). We need both the Word and prayer, God's speech to us and our speech to him so that we will know his love for us and that we can express ours to him.

This phrase "praying in the Holy Spirit" is one of those misunderstood phrases in the New Testament, in my opinion, as one having been converted in the Charismatic and Pentecostal movements. What does this mean? The most popular understanding in much of evangelical Christianity is that it means speaking in "tongues" (1 Corinthians 12; 14). What is striking to me as I study this language is that when the New Testament exhorts us to pray "in the Spirit," it is always in the context of ordinary prayer, not the supposed ecstatic tongues. For example, in Ephesians 6:18 Paul says that we are to pray "in the Spirit." The context is not only standing up against all the assaults of the devil but also praying for his preaching while he was in prison. This does not mean that it is rote and perfunctory. It means that it is prayer in dependence and reliance on the Holy Spirit to help us. As Bede said, "We pray in the Holy Spirit when we are moved by divine inspiration to ask for heavenly help, so that we may receive the good things which we cannot obtain on our own."[133]

---

132 *James, 1–2 Peter, 1–3 John, Jude*, ed. Bray, 257.
133 *James, 1–2 Peter, 1–3 John, Jude*, ed. Bray, 257.

What Jude is saying here is that our strength to engage the contention of the faith comes through the means of persevering prayer that grabs hold of God's promises of love for us even as we express our love for him. Why does he mention prayer so closely to the Holy Spirit? It is to stir us up from our spiritual slumber. Are we to be busy in prayer? Yes. But it's not prayer that arises from the human spirit but that arises from the divine Person of the Holy Spirit. We know we need to pray as Christians. And there are times when our conscience says to us, "You need to pray." That's the Holy Spirit. He leads us through his Word and in prompting our conscience in ways consistent with the Word to pray. What Jude is saying is that we are to be in prayer that is informed by the Spirit. We pray in accord with the things we find in the Word of God. We find the words to pray, even, in the Word. What Jude is saying is that we are to be in prayer that is in dependence upon the Spirit. We rely on him as God to take our feeble prayers and make them his own before the throne of grace. "From the Spirit we receive the gift of real concern, ardour, forcefulness, eagerness, confidence that we shall receive—all these, and finally those groanings which cannot be uttered, as Paul writes (Romans 8.26)."[134]

Waiting

The fourth and final key to our contention is to "keep yourselves in the love of God" by "waiting for the mercy of our Lord Jesus Christ that leads to eternal life" (v. 21). "Remembering," "building," and "praying." What do those verbs have in common? They are all energetic. But now Jude uses a more restful verb: "waiting." Yes we are to be alert and expectant for this coming of the Lord, but it is more of a resignation that he is coming and a calmness because of that. Paul describes the new life of the believer as a "turn[ing] to God from

---

134 Calvin, *Commentary*, 335.

idols" (1 Thessalonians 1:9a). And when we are turned around on the road of life, we energetically "serve the living and true God" as well as calmly "wait for his Son from heaven, whom he raised from the dead, Jesus who delivers us from the wrath to come" (1 Thessalonians 1:9b–10). And when Jesus comes as our "blessed hope" (Titus 2:13) we will experience by sight his abundant mercy that we now can only experience and wait for by faith.

Yet we've all heard the adage, "I don't want to be so heavenly minded that I am of no earthly good." And that would seem to apply here, especially since we are to be contending. How would lifting up our hearts to heaven for Jesus help us in the here and now? This is a key to our contention because unless you are heavenly minded you can be no earthly good to the world that is lost in sin. You can be used for earthly good precisely because you are heavenly minded. It's because you are awaiting this mercy of Christ at his Second Coming that you now are experiencing the preserving power of God's love to you, which motivates you to contend for the faith.

Conclusion

We have a huge war in front of us: contend against false doctrine and contend for the souls of the world. Who is sufficient for these things? Surely none of us. But God calls us to preparation like soldiers. He calls us to exercise ourselves in remembering the Word. He calls us to become more and more secure in his love for us and our love for him. Prepare yourselves for this task so that you can sincerely be used of him to bring the gospel to the needy.

8
The Calm in the Storm

Jude 24–25

ᔆ   ᔆ

AT the beginning of the massive and decisive Battle of the Pelennor Fields in J.R.R. Tolkien's, *The Return of the King*, tens of thousands of evil orcs of the Dark Lord Sauron are besieging the white city of Minas Tirith, capital of the kingdom of Gondor, defended by just several thousand men. As the city gate was breached, fires were raging all around, and hope seemed to wane, then in the distance was heard the sound of horns. Gondor had stood alone, but not for long. When the cavalry of the neighboring kingdom of Rohan come to aid, though, there are but 6,000 Rohirrim (riders of Rohan). These faced a field of tens of thousands stretched across an expanse. Bolstered by their king Théoden's command "in a loud voice, more clear than any there had ever heard a mortal man achieve before," the ride of the

Rohirrim commenced. And as they charged and engaged the enemy in this great clash of metal and flesh, we read an unexpected line:

> And then all the host of Rohan burst into song, and they sang as they slew, for the joy of the battle was on them, and the sound of their singing that was fair and terrible came even to the City.[135]

"They sang as they slew." Amidst the clanging conflict, there was the sound of joyful song. What an image for us to consider here at the end of Jude's neglected letter. As I said in the Preface, while we are contending for the faith (v. 3), against false teachers (vv. 4–16), and for the sake of confused and lost souls (vv. 17–23), we are to be content in the Lord who loves us (v. 1).

To put it in an image you may be more familiar with, imagine a hurricane you've seen on the news or online—or maybe up close and personal. As a Californian, I've only seen the images of devastation that comes from a hurricane. But we all know how the strength is measured by the speed of the winds: category 1, up to 95 miles (153 kilometers) per hour, or category 5, 157 miles (252 kilometers) per hour and above. We know how much rain comes down in a hurricane causing massive floods. We know how high the waves get along the coast, devastating homes and businesses. In a word, a hurricane is chaos. Yet, in the middle of the hurricane, known as the eye, there is an ironic calm. While everything else is in chaos, there is the surreal reality of the calmness in the eye.

The church of Jesus Christ exists today as it has always existed in the midst of such spiritual chaos of a fallen world. There is the constant threat from the world to persecute the church, to silence the church, and to extinguish the light of the church by infiltrating it and

---

135 J.R.R. Tolkien, *The Return of the King* (1955; Second edition, Boston, MA: Houghton Mifflin Company, 1965), Book 5:113.

perverting its message. There is the constant struggle of a life affected by sin, as we are tempted to give ear to false prophets and to sear our consciences against the Lordship of Jesus over our lives. There is the constant onslaught of Satan's fiery arrows (Ephesians 6:16), seeking to destroy our faith and send us to hell. All of this chaos surrounds us even while we are seeking to contend for the faith and to save sinners from eternal destruction.

So where do we find our calm in the midst of this satanic storm? According to Jude 24–25 we find calm in the God whom we worship. Jude concludes his letter with a doxology, that is, words of praise to God. It's always been this way. While the family line of Cain was known for its worldly exploits of building cities, herding livestock, creating instruments and playing music, and forging weapons of bronze and iron (Genesis 4:17–24), the family line of Seth was known for calling upon the name of the Lord in worship (Genesis 4:26). After seeing the plagues upon Egypt, leaving by night, being chased into the desert, crossing the Red Sea only to see the Egyptians drowned in dramatic fashion, what did Israel do? They sang: "I will sing to the LORD, for he has triumphed gloriously; the horse and his rider he has thrown into the sea" (Exodus 15:1). When the infant New Covenant church experienced persecution and the arrest of its two most prominent leaders, Peter and John, they all met for worship and prayer after their release (Acts 3–4). Later, Herod had James killed while Peter and other Christians were arrested (Acts 12:1–4). While in prison, "earnest prayer for him was made to God by the church" (Acts 12:5). And when an angel miraculously released him from prison, where did he go? He went to Mary's house where a prayer meeting was underway (Acts 12:12). When Paul and Silas were beaten and imprisoned for exorcising a demon-possessed girl, causing the idol stock market to plummet, we hear them in the innermost prison cell "praying and singing hymns to God" (Acts 16:25). While John was exiled on the island of Patmos "on account of the word of God and the testimony of Jesus" he says he was "in the Spirit on the Lord's day" (Revelation 1:9–10), meaning, he was praying and worshiping.

The church of Jesus Christ was redeemed to be a worshipping church. Like our forefathers and foremothers in Israel, we exist as "a chosen race, a royal priesthood, a holy nation, a people for his own possession" for this great purpose: "that you may proclaim the excellencies of him who called you out of darkness into his marvelous light" (1 Peter 2:9).[136] To this all believers will say "Amen!" But more importantly for our purpose here, the church is a worshipping church in the midst of the chaotic spiritual war we are involved in. And in that chaos, the worship of our Triune God of grace gives us calm that the world cannot understand, a "peace … which surpasses all understanding" (Philippians 4:7).

The God We Worship

First, Jude's doxology expresses our contentedness in the conflict of faith by describing the God we worship. He opens this doxological conclusion with, "Now to him who is able" (v. 24). Who is this "him?" Verse 25 continues: "to the only God, our Savior, through Jesus Christ our Lord." Before Jude says anything in praise for what God has done for us or for the world he simply praises him for who he is in himself. He is "worthy to be praised" (Psalm 18:3). The Triune God deserves our praise for who he is before we praise him for what he does. We see this in the worship of heaven:

> And the four living creatures, each of them with six wings, are full of eyes all around and within, and day and night they never

---

136 On this theme, see Daniel R. Hyde, *God in Our Midst: The Tabernacle and Our Relationship with God* (Orlando: Reformation Trust, 2012), 4–5.

cease to say, "Holy, holy, holy, is the Lord God Almighty, who was and is and is to come!" (Revelation 4:8)

Worthy are you, our Lord and God, to receive glory and honor and power, for you created all things, and by your will they existed and were created. (Revelation 4:11)

Isn't this so important in our day when worship is turned into entertainment, into a venue, into a destination, and into a thing we utilize to feel better, get blessed, and feel close to God? Worship exists for the glorification of God not the satisfaction of our desires.

So who is the God we are to worship? Jude has already called him "God the Father," which obviously means he has a Son, our Lord Jesus Christ (vv. 1, 4). Jude has said that God is a gracious God (v. 3), a loving God (vv. 1, 21), and a merciful God (v. 21) who saves his people (vv. 5, 25). He's also a just God of wrath and righteousness (vv. 5, 6, 7, 14, 15).

Now he calls him the God "who is able." This is a frequent theme in New Testament doxologies: "Now to him who is able to strengthen you according to my gospel and the preaching of Jesus Christ" (Romans 16:25); "Now to him who is able to do far more abundantly than all that we ask or think" (Ephesians 3:20). What is it meant to communicate that God is "able?" It says to us in the fight of faith, where there are gains and losses, victories and defeats, that our God is almighty and sovereign over all things. And because he is such an Almighty God, the Heidelberg Catechism says we benefit because "whatever evil he sends upon me in this troubled life, He will turn to my good; for He is able to do it, being Almighty God, and willing also, being a faithful Father" (HC, Q&A 26). What can be more calming in the conflict than that thought? We need to hear this again and again in all the cultural and political conflicts we face.

We also rest content to know that we worship and serve "the only God, our Savior, through Jesus Christ our Lord" (v. 25). We do not worship the idols of the nations, which are the works of human hands and therefore unable to speak, see, hear, smell, feel, and walk like our God (Psalm 115:4–8). We worship the one true God who eternally exists as Father, Son, and Holy Spirit in self-sufficient and self-satisfying love and who is also the God who has revealed himself in his holy and divine Word.

This is so important for us to realize today. The idols of our world are pleasure. But pleasure is fading. The idols of our world are power. But power only leads to realizing there is someone more powerful. The idols of our world are prestige. But prestige is never enough. Only God is, and is therefore sufficient. Worship him for who he is.

And this true God is not only a God who exists "out there"—he is "our Savior." How can we make such a claim? Because the God who is, saves us "through Jesus Christ our Lord." Jesus Christ is the eternal Son of God who took to himself a true human nature. And as this co-eternal God he has come down to our level in our humanity to make the Heavenly Father known to us. As John says so astonishingly, "No one has ever seen God; the only God, who is at the Father's side, he has made him known" (John 1:18). No one can see God and live (Exodus 33:20; Isaiah 6:5). He exists in the unapproachable light of his own glory and holiness (1 Timothy 6:16); we are sinners. Do the math! But since this one glorious God exists as three co-equal, co-glorious persons—Father, Son, and Holy Spirit—one of those persons, God the Son, came to earth by becoming a man. And John says he did this to make the Father, whom he knew in intimacy being at his side for all eternity, known to us. What a God! He deserves our worship!

The Reason We Worship

As we worship this God, he alone is enough to give us calm in the storm against the faith. But Jude connects the God we worship with the reason we worship him, saying, "Now to him who is able *to keep you from stumbling* and *to present you blameless before the presence of his glory* with great joy" (v. 24). We worship an Almighty God in which exists all potential and actual power. And Jude says he applies that towards us in two ways: one way benefits us in this life and the other way benefits us in the life to come.

We worship God because in this life he is able "to keep you from stumbling" (v. 24). As we gather together as congregations of the Lord Jesus Christ, there are some who are going to come in and try to pervert the grace that liberates from sin by making it into license to sin (v. 4). God is able to keep us from stumbling into this error. There are some whose lives are actually going to evidence that they have fallen into sin (v. 23). But God is able to keep us from stumbling so that we can minister to them and bring them out. All of us are going to be tempted with the allure of sin. But God is able to keep us from stumbling and falling flat on our faces into that life.

This teaches us about the grace of God in preserving his people until the end, or, the perseverance of the saints. Perseverance is just as much a gift of God as our being justified in the first place. The Canons of Dort summarizes the graciousness of God's preserving grace when it says that while Christians are prone to sin and can even fall into sins in this life, "it is not in consequence of their own merits or strength, but of God's free mercy, that they neither totally fall from faith and grace nor continue and perish finally in their backslidings" (CD 5.8). This article goes on to say that if left to us, this would happen; but because it is based in God himself, it is impossible. There are several biblical reasons. First, God's "counsel cannot be changed nor His promise fail" (CD 5.8). Since God does not change (Malachi 3:6) neither do his counsel or promises (Psalm 33:11). Second, God's "call according to His purpose [cannot] be revoked" (CD 5.8). As Paul says concerning elect Jews, "the gifts and the calling of God are irrevocable" (Romans 11:29). Third, the "merit, intercession, and preservation of Christ [cannot] be rendered ineffectual." By Jesus' merit, that is, his obedient life culminating in the cross (Romans 5:18–19), he secured for us an eternal redemption (Hebrews 9:12). By his intercessory prayers, Peter's faith did not fail (Luke 22:31–34) and by those same prayers he is able to save us to the uttermost (Hebrews 7:25). And by his preserving power, not even the devil can snatch us from his hand (John 10:28–30). And fourth, "the sealing of the Holy Spirit [cannot] be frustrated or obliterated" (CD 5.8). As Paul says, we have been sealed with the Holy Spirit as the guarantee that we will one day acquire full possession of our inheritance (Ephesians 1:13–14). The reason we worship this God is that he is "worthy to be praised" (Psalm 18:3) because of what he does for us.

We worship God because in the life to come he is able "to present you blameless before the presence of his glory with great joy" (v. 24). In this life we are constantly being stained by sin. But God is able to bring us into his glorious presence spotless. As Ephesians 1:4 says God chose us in Christ so that "we should be holy and blameless before him." Colossians 1:22 says Jesus died for this purpose so that he would "present you holy and blameless and above reproach before him." And Ephesians 5:27 says this as well. Jesus laid down his life as a husband for his bride, "so that he might present the church to himself in splendor, without spot or wrinkle or any such thing, that she might be holy and without blemish." As one hymn celebrates this truth:

May she soon all glorious be,
Spotless and from wrinkle free,

Pure, and bright, and worthy Thee.
We beseech thee, hear us.[137]

That moment will be one of "great joy" (v. 24). David once prayed that in the Lord's presence there was "fullness of joy" (Psalm 16:11). We contend and labor and strive now with that joy set out before us. We do so with our Lord blazing the trail for us as the first one who also labored in this life to enter the rest to come. We are called to "lay aside every weight, and sin which clings so closely" and to "run with endurance the race that is set before us" (Hebrews 12:1). How? "Looking to Jesus, the founder and perfecter of our faith, who *for the joy that was set before him* endured the cross, despising the shame, and is seated at the right hand of the throne of God" (Hebrews 12:2). That joy awaits us when we hear the words, "Well done, good and faithful servant. You have been faithful over a little; I will set you over much. Enter into the joy of your master" (Matthew 25:21, 23).

The Vocabulary of Our Worship

As we have to contend with those who speak "harsh things ... against [the Lord]" (v. 15), how are we to worship him in a holy way—or, how older writers spoke: "holily?" Our words matter. How we speak of God matters. In a church like mine, we hear the Ten Commandments read almost every Sunday morning. And we hear the words of the third commandment, "You shall not take the name of the LORD you God in vain, for the LORD will not hold him guiltless who takes his name in vain" (Exodus 20:7). Positively, this commandment is requiring of us that we "use the holy name of God in no other way than with fear and reverence, so that He might be rightly confessed and worshipped by us, and be glorified in all our words and works" (HC, Q&A 99).

How do we worship the one true God for his preserving grace in

---

137 From the hymn, "Jesus, With Thy Church Abide," by Thomas Benson Pollock.

this life and the life to come? Jude gives us in verse 25 a vocabulary of worship. He says we are to ascribe to our blessed God "glory, majesty, dominion, and authority, before all time and now and forever. Amen."

God deserves "glory," that is, supreme weight and worth. He is everything; he deserves everything. When we worship him in thoughts, words, and deeds, we are not to hold just a little back for ourselves. Give it all to him.

God deserves "majesty," that is, that regal splendor of a king. He is not to be approached flippantly and lightly. We are to "serve [him] with fear and rejoice [in him] with trembling" (Psalm 2:11) because he is a King who exists as a "consuming fire" (Hebrews 12:29).

God deserves "dominion," that is, supreme Lordship over every single square inch in the universe and over every last thought in our minds. Since he made every square inch and rules over every square inch in his powerful and tender providence, he deserves everything we have to give.

God deserves "authority," that is, the final say in "all things that pertain to life and godliness" (2 Peter 1:3) so that he is glorified and we are edified. How can he deserve anything less?

And he deserves all this, and everything imaginable, "before all time and now and forever." What does it mean to say God is eternal? The best way to wrap our finite minds around this is to say he was, and is, and is to come. He existed in eternity past, he existed in eternity present, and he will exist in eternity future. So when we say he is worthy of praise he deserves our praise in every time and in every realm of eternity.

The final word of worship Jude gives us is that short biblical word, "Amen." So small, yet so majestic. This is our response of "Yes!" to all

God is, all God has said in his Word, all God does in our lives, and all God will do for the life of the world. And even though this is my affirmation, it is offered because of who God is. As the Heidelberg Catechism concludes:

What is the meaning of the word "Amen"?

"Amen" means: so shall it truly and surely be. For my prayer is much more certainly heard of God than I feel in my heart that I desire these things of Him. (HC, Q&A 129)

How fitting is that word for the end of this letter? The church is under attack from stealth soldiers of Satan. The Word of God is under attack. People's faith is under attack. God's own existence and Lordship over all is under attack. But God is able to finish the work he started in the beginning, in a lowly manger, on a heinous cross, and in an empty tomb. May it be so, O Lord!

Conclusion

The world is a hurricane. Worship is the eye in the midst of the hurricane. Every week come out of the chaos and enter the peace of public worship with other brothers and sisters. And then go back out into the storm to fight against the winds of false doctrine. That's Jude's message. One hymn writer once wrote these beautiful words that express the calm in the storm that we experience through worshipping our great God:

In perfect peace the clouds I view,
The gathering storm I see,
For Thou hast taught my soul to know
It shall be well with me.

In perfect peace, O gracious Lord,
Till life's last hour shall close,

I'll sing Thy goodness o'er and o'er,
And on Thy love repose.[138]

---

138 From the hymn, "Perfect Peace," by Fanny Crosby.

Bibliography

Aalders, G. Ch. *Genesis: Volume I*, trans. William Heynen, Bible Student's Commentary (Grand Rapids: Zondervan, 1981).

Allberry, Sam. *Is God Anti-Gay? And Other Questions About Homosexuality, the Bible and Same-Sex Attraction* (Epsom: The Good Book Company, 2013).

Allen, Joel S. "A New Possibility for the Three-Clause Format of Jude 22–3." *New Testament Studies* 44:1 (1998): 133–143.

Bandstra. Andrew J. "Onward Christian Soldiers—Praying in Love, with Mercy: Preaching on the Epistle of Jude." *Calvin Theological Journal* 32 (1997): 136–139.

Bauckham, Richard J. *Jude, 2 Peter*, Word Biblical Commentary (Waco, TX: Word, 1983).

_____, *Jude and the Relatives of Jesus in the Early Church* (Edinburgh: T. & T. Clark, 1990.

Baucham, Voddie. "Contending for the Faith." As found at http://www.sermonaudio.com/sermoninfo.asp?SID=5309038320.

Black, Matthew. "The Maranatha Invocation and Jude 14, 15 (1 Enoch 1:9)," in *Christ and the Spirit in the New Testament*, ed. Barnabas Lindars and Stephen S. Smalley (Cambridge, U.K.: Cambridge University Press, 1973).

Bray, Gerald L. ed. *James, 1–2 Peter, 1–3 John, Jude*, Ancient Christian Commentary on Scripture: New Testament, Volume XI, (Downers Grove, IL: InterVarsity Press, 2000).

Bruce, F. F. *The Canon of Scripture* (Downers Grove, Ill.: InterVarsity Press, 1988).

Calvin, John. *A Harmony of the Gospels Matthew, Mark and Luke, Volume 3, and the Epistles of James and Jude*, trans. A. W. Morrison, eds. David W. Torrance and Thomas F. Torrance, Calvin's New Testament Commentaries, 12 vols. Grand Rapids, Mich.: Eerdmans, 1972.

_____, "John Calvin's 1542 Exposition of Jude." Translated by Thomas and Geneviève Reid. *Kerux: The Journal of Northwest Theological Seminary* 26/3 (2011): 3–15. As found at http://www.kerux.com/doc/2603A1.asp.

Charles, J. Daryl. *2 Peter, Jude* in *1–2 Peter, Jude*, Believers Church Bible Commentary (Scottdale, PA: Herald Press, 1999).

_____, "Jude's Use of Pseudepigraphical Source-Material as Part of a Literary Strategy." *New Testament Studies* 37:1 (January 1991): 130–145.

_____, "Literary Artifice in the Epistle of Jude." *Zeitschrift für die Neutestamentliche Wissenschaft und die Kunde der Älteren Kirche* 82 (January 1, 1991): 106–124.

Clement of Alexandria, "Comments on the Epistle of Jude," in *Ante-Nicene Fathers*, trans. William Wilson, 10 vols. (1885; repr., Peabody, MA: Hendrickson Publishers, Inc., fourth printing 2004).

Comfort, Philip Wesley. *A Commentary on the Manuscripts and Text of the New Testament* (Grand Rapids, MI: Kregel Academic, 2015).

DeYoung, Kevin. *What Does the Bible Really Teach About Homosexuality?* (Wheaton, IL: Crossway, 2015).

Ferguson, Sinclair. *The Whole Christ: Legalism, Antinomianism, & Gospel Assurance—Why the Marrow Controversy Still Matters* (Wheaton, IL: Crossway, 2016).

Gagnon, Robert A. J. *The Bible and Homosexual Practice: Texts and Hermeneutics* (Nashville, TN: Abingdon Press, 2001).

Green, Gene L. *Jude and 2 Peter*, Baker Exegetical Commentary on the New Testament (Grand Rapids: Baker Academic, 2008).

Green, Michael. *The Second Epistle General of Peter and the General Epistle of Jude*, Tyndale New Testament Commentaries (Grand Rapids, MI: Eerdmans, 1968).

House, Paul R. "Examining the Narrative of Old Testament Narrative: An Exploration in Biblical Theology." *Westminster Theological Journal* 67:2 (Fall 2005): 229–245.

Hyde, Daniel R. *From the Pen of Pastor Paul: 1–2 Thessalonians* (Welwyn Garden City, UK: EP Books, 2015).

_____, *God in Our Midst: The Tabernacle and Our Relationship with God* (Orlando: Reformation Trust, 2012).

_____, *Welcome to a Reformed Church: A Guide for Pilgrims* (2010; Orlando, FL: Reformation Trust, fourth printing 2015).

Jones, Hywel. "The Value of an Unwritten Letter (Part 1)." *The Outlook* 50:11 (December 2000): 5–6.

_____, "The Value of an Unwritten Letter (Part 2)." *The Outlook* 51:1 (January 2001): 18.

Jones, Mark. *Antinomianism: Reformed Theology's Unwelcome Guest?* (Phillipsburg: P&R Publishing, 2013).

Joubert, Stephan J. "Persuasion in the Letter of Jude." *The Journal for the Study of the New Testament* 58 (1995): 75–87.

Kelly, J.N.D. *A Commentary on the Epistles of Peter and of Jude* (New York: Harper & Row, 1969).

Kistemaker, Simon J. *Exposition of the Epistles of Peter and of the Epistle of Jude*, New Testament Commentary (1987; Grand Rapids, MI: Baker Book House, second printing 1988).

Lane, William L. *The Gospel of Mark*, The New International Commentary on the New Testament (Grand Rapids, MI: William B. Eerdmans Publishing Company, 1974).

Lucas, Dick and Christopher Green. *The Message of 2 Peter & Jude: The Promise of His Coming*. The Bible Speaks Today (Leicester, England/Downers Grove, IL: Inter-Varsity Press, 1995).

Luther, Martin. "Sermons on the Epistle of St. Jude," trans. Martin H. Bertram, in *Luther's Works: Volume 30, Catholic Epistles*, ed. Jaroslav Pelikan (Saint Louis, MO: Concordia Publishing House, 1967).

Manton, Thomas, *A Practical Commentary, or An Exposition with Notes on the Epistle of Jude* in *The Works of Thomas Manton: Volume 5* (Birmingham, AL: Solid Ground Christian Books, 2008).

Martin, Ralph P. "Jude," in Andrew Chester and Ralph P. Martin, *The Theology of the Letters of James, Peter, and Jude*, New Testament Theology (1994; repr., Cambridge: Cambridge University Press, 1996).

Metzger, Bruce. *A Textual Commentary on the Greek New Testament* (corrected edition; London: United Bible Societies, 1975).

Moo, Douglas J. *2 Peter and Jude*, The NIV Application Commentary (Grand Rapids, MI: Zondervan Publishing House, 1996).

Osburn, Carroll D. "The Text of Jude 5." *Biblica* 62:1 (1981): 107–115.

Poole, Matthew. *The Exegetical Labors of the Reverend Matthew Poole, Volume 79: 1 John–Jude*, trans. Steven Dilday, ed. April M. McLeod (Culpeper, VA: Master Poole Publishing, 2013).

Richards, E. Randolph. *Paul and First-Century Letter Writing: Secretaries, Composition and Collection* (Downers Grove, IL: IVP Academic, 2004).

Ridderbos, Herman N. *Redemptive History and the New Testament Scriptures*, trans. H. De Jongste, rev. Richard B. Gaffin, Jr., Biblical & Theological Studies (1963; second rev. ed., Phillipsburg, N.J.: Presbyterian and Reformed, 1988).

Rowston, D.J. "The Most Neglected Book in the New Testament." *New Testament Studies* 21:4 (July 1975): 554–563.

Schreiner, Thomas R. *1, 2 Peter, Jude*, The New American Commentary: Volume 37 (Nashville, TN: Broadman & Holman Publishers, 2003).

Stott, John R. W. *The Message of Romans*, The Bible Speaks Today (Downers Grove, IL: Inter-Varsity Press, 1994).

Stuart, Douglas. "Malachi," in *The Minor Prophets: An Exegetical & Expository Commentary*, 3 vols. (Grand Rapids: Baker Books, 2003).

The Gospel & Sexual Orientation: A Testimony of the Reformed Presbyterian Church of North America (Pittsburg: Crown & Covenant Publications and The Synod of the Reformed Presbyterian Church of North America, 2012).

Trapp, John. *A Commentary or Exposition Upon All the Epistles and the Revelation of John the Divine* (London, 1647).

Waltke, Bruce K. *Genesis: A Commentary* (Grand Rapids: Zondervan, 2001).

Watson, Duane Frederick. *Invention, Arrangement, and Style: Rhetorical Criticism of Jude and 2 Peter*, SBLDS 104 (Atlanta, GA: Scholar's Press, 1998).

Wheaton, David H. "Jude," in *The New Bible Commentary: Revised*, ed. D. Guthrie and J.A. Motyer (Grand Rapids: Eerdmans, 1970).